All-Around-the-House
ART *and* CRAFT *Book*

All-Around-the-House ART and CRAFT Book

by Patricia Z. Wirtenberg

Photographs by Patricia Z. Wirtenberg

HOUGHTON MIFFLIN COMPANY BOSTON

Lovingly to Mom and Dad... and, especially, to my husband who envisioned, encouraged, and enjoyed. Life, with Lee, is *good*.

___

ISBN 0-395-07209-3 hardbound
ISBN 0-395-19974-3 paperbound
Copyright © 1968 by Patricia A. Wirtenberg
All Rights Reserved Including the Right
to Reproduce This Book or Parts Thereof in Any Form
Library of Congress Catalog Card Number: 68-28058
Printed in the U. S. A.

Fourth Printing H,M

CONTENTS

PREFACE

LEARNING to create works of art from materials in your own house can be both inexpensive and fun for you. A young person of any age can do it, and it doesn't have to be a complicated, expensive or formal process. It can be easygoing, eye-opening and taste-expanding as you begin to see old things in a new light, as you begin to arrange and relate ordinary things in an extraordinary way. You'll understand form when you begin to work with the unnoticed shape of a detergent bottle or a vegetable container. You'll feel texture when you touch wood and wool with a new awareness. Colors will come alive when you search for them in foodstuffs and fallen leaves.

Just look around you! That's the first and most important step in creating an artist's environment for yourself. You don't need a country barn or a garret with a skylight. You don't need oil paints and canvas. Imagination, ideas, a searching attitude and the materials of ordinary life — those are the things that an artist really works with. In *The All-Around-the-House Art Book*, those are the things that you will work with.

The projects in this book have been designed to help you to explore your way into the artist's world, to experiment with the materials you find and to enjoy the fun and excitement of creating art all-around-the-house. You don't need to buy any special artists' materials; almost everything you need is already somewhere near you.

So look around the home you live in, whether it is a three-story house, or a three-room apartment. Look into your attic (in an apartment, your "attic" may be a storage chest or a catch-all upper shelf in a closet). Look into the garage, the kitchen, the laundry and the backyard.

From whatever you find — old newspapers, chicken bones, shoe polish, egg cartons, soap powders, fabrics, hangers and starch — you'll make paintings, collages, mosaics, prints and sculpture.

And in this process of trying, experimenting and doing, you'll discover the joy of creating art with materials that are all-around-the-house.

All-Around-the-House
ART *and* CRAFT *Book*

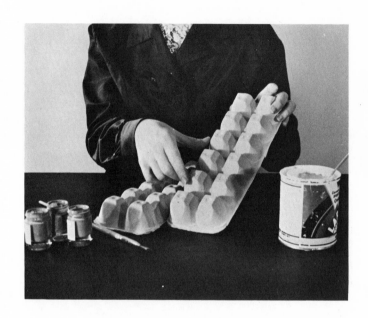

PAINTED EGG CARTONS

a study of color arrangement in three dimensions

LOOK AT ANY egg carton. Study a single section for holding one egg and you will see that it has eight or more sides. If you then count the connecting areas of the carton between the individual egg cup sections, you will see that the carton is an interesting arrangement of many separate surfaces.

If you were planning to design such an arrangement of surfaces and found an interesting pattern was already available to you in the form of an egg carton, your "work" is half done!

The idea of this project is to create a visual arrangement by painting each surface a separate color. The colors that are next to one another must be related and, with so many sides to paint, it takes planning to see that two side-by-side areas don't end up with the same color. You'll discover that the painting step itself is not very difficult, but the planning of where the colors go, before you begin to paint, takes time.

You'll need three or more colors for painting. These few colors can then be mixed to give you many more

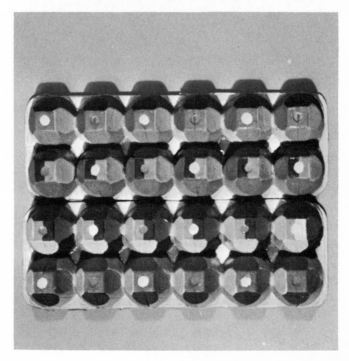

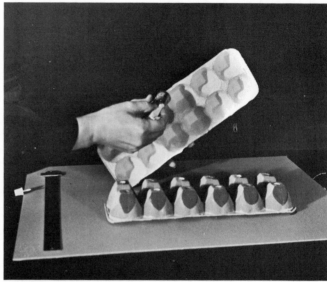

colors. You'll also need glue and a flat piece of card-board if you wish to mount your finished painted egg carton. (I prefer to work on two egg cartons at one time for it makes my finished piece larger and more important.)

If you begin to paint by choosing one color and painting the same side of all the egg sections this color, your work will go smoothly. Once the first color is painted, wash your brush and go on with the second color. Keep changing colors until all the sides and connecting areas are painted.

The paint will dry quickly on the absorbent card-board material of the egg carton. When each carton is dry you can then glue it onto a large sheet of cardboard.

The colors you have chosen and the design you have made by your arrangement of those colors on the many surfaces of the carton will give it a "personality" of its own. Is it gay or is it serious? Is it loud or quiet? Try painting more cartons using other color schemes to create an entirely different egg carton "personality"!

CUBE ART

transforming sugar cubes with paint

FOR THIS PROJECT you will need a box of notched sugar cubes, thick poster paints (or house paints) in three or four colors, gold or silver paint, fast-drying glue, a sheet of plywood or *very* stiff cardboard for the background, and some sandpaper.

To begin, snap dozens of sugar cubes in half at the notch. Mix the three or four starting colors in various combinations with each other so that you have many more colors. Such mixing always produces colors that are harmoniously related to one another.

Paint the sides of each cube a color and then paint its top a contrasting color. Try as many side and top combinations as you can imagine. Leave the bottom side of the cube unpainted; it will be later glued to the background. You may want to paint a few cubes all gold or all silver. These metal-colored cubes will add a "sparkle" to your finished wall relief.

When the paint has dried, you can begin to assemble your creation. First of all, measure and mark the center of your background. Start your Cube Art at this point and work from the center out toward both sides and toward the top and bottom. Leave a wide border on all

four sides, with the bottom border being slightly wider than the other three. This will be your frame area.

The sugar cubes are glued on in horizontal and vertical rows. Glue some of the unpainted bottom sides flat against the background, but glue the others at angles so that their painted sides show. Occasionally you will need to sandpaper a corner to glue the angled cubes firmly to the board. The more irregular the surface is the more interesting it will be. Light will catch on this bumpy surface and it will be far more beautiful than if all the pieces are applied flat.

While you are in the process of gluing, you must also remember that you are composing a pleasing color design. Isn't it more interesting if you avoid the ordinary pattern of a checkerboard which puts light colors next to dark colors? Instead, similar colors can be grouped together. You can also insert a gold or silver cube here and there for added variety. End your gluing with edges that are straight on all four sides. This border will frame your finished Cube Art. Select one of your darkest colors and paint the frame area.

Once you have mastered the technique, you may want to experiment with a circular or diagonal arrangement of cubes.

VEGETABLE PRINTING

printing with fruits and vegetables

THERE ARE NUMEROUS ways of making prints, some more complicated or expensive than others. Vegetable Printing is one of the simplest, best-known and least expensive of all printing methods.

You can use any hard vegetable or fruit such as a potato, turnip, carrot, apple, radish, onion or pear. You'll also need a knife, some scrap paper for experimenting and some better paper for printing. The printing "ink" is poster paint.

Begin by cutting your fruit or vegetable into slices or wedges of varying sizes—large or small, thick or thin. Then use your knife to dig out a simple design on the face of the slice. You might even try notching or scalloping its edges. You can design or decorate the vegetable slice a lot or a little. You may want to leave a slice or two plain and undecorated if you like its shape just the way it is.

When you have a few pieces ready, you can start printing. Select one interesting slice and apply paint to the face of it, keeping the paint fairly thick. First, press your slice to scrap paper. Lift it without wiggling it on the paper. Remember that printing is an up-and-down motion. If you push or drag your vegetable, you'll blur the color and smear the print. When you want to change colors, either use another piece of vegetable or wash the one that you are using.

Try some different effects: mix two colors directly on the slice by painting one half one color and the other half another color; use the edges of very thin slices to print; try printing one shape over another and one color over another.

When you've experimented enough on scrap paper, try printing on a better piece of paper. You can print an abstract design or you can print a realistic picture. It's up to you!

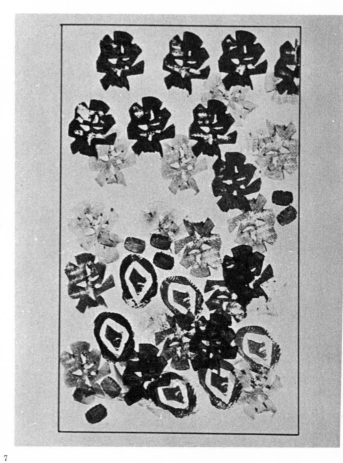

TINFOIL ENGRAVING

a way of denting a smooth surface

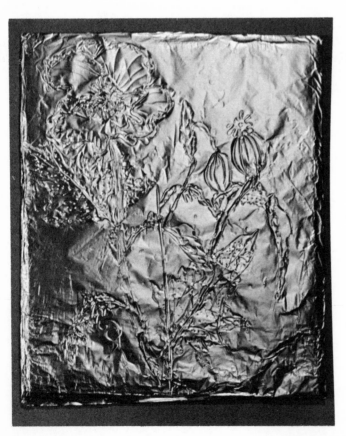

THE IDEA OF TINFOIL ENGRAVING is to draw on the foil with a pointed tool which is sharp enough to dent the surface of the foil but dull or rounded enough not to cut through it.

The materials you will need are tinfoil, a stiff piece of cardboard, some newspaper, cellophane tape and some "engraving" tools such as a knitting needle, a large nail or the handle end of a spoon.

Tear or cut several sheets of newspaper to the size of the piece of cardboard. Tear off a large sheet of tinfoil so that when it is doubled, it will be larger than the cardboard by several inches. Double the foil and place it on top of the pad of newspaper. Doubling the foil and cushioning it underneath with newspaper will help to prevent your tool from cutting through the foil. Secure the foil in place by wrapping the edges behind the cardboard and taping them to the back. Smooth out any wrinkles with your hands. The tinfoil surface is now ready for engraving.

Draw your picture with your tool directly onto the foil. Work carefully, for lines once engraved cannot be easily "erased." Experiment with lines made by different tools. A knitting needle makes a line entirely different from that made by a key or your fingernail.

Try to draw with long, connected strokes for short broken lines look ragged and unsure. Use finer tools for finer details after using more blunt, broader tools for large outlines.

When you frame your Tinfoil Engraving, be careful not to press down on the face of the engraving as you fit the frame or the engraved lines will be flattened and their detail dulled.

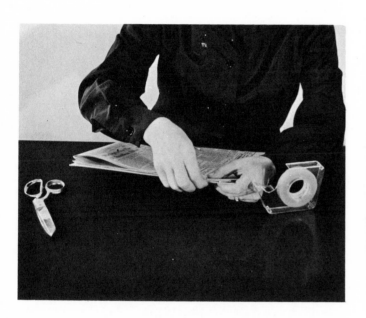

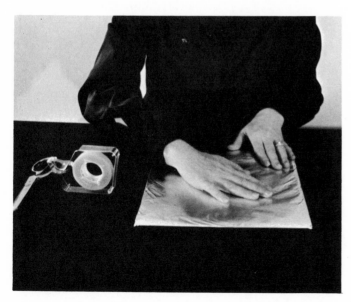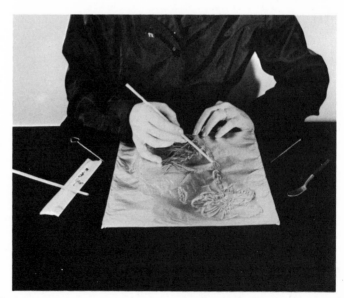

CALCIUM COLLAGE

a picture made from bones and shells

THIS AMUSING COLLAGE starts from one special kind of leftover. Of course, you'll have to rescue this art material before any one else disposes of it as "garbage." The leftovers can be poultry or meat bones and crab, clam, oyster or lobster shells. You can even include eggshells. You'll also need a stiff background in a dark, rich color and some fast-drying glue.

Bones will be found in many shapes. They can be small, medium or large, thick or thin. Shells are even more varied in size and shape. They will probably add more color to your collage than bones, especially if they include the red-orange of boiled lobster and crab shells.

First, wash and dry all your materials thoroughly. Seashells should be washed in soapy water to rid them of their fishy odor. Bones can be dried in the air or in an oven.

Start your picture by placing some bones and shells on your background and then experiment with different arrangements. This arranging and rearranging is very important, for you are letting the materials themselves suggest the idea and the composition of your picture. That's exactly the way many contemporary artists work.

When you've arranged a picture that pleases you,

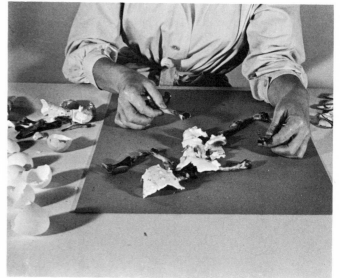

you can start to glue the pieces onto the background. Pick up each bone or shell, one by one, and apply glue to its edge. Place it back into the composition.

Don't limit yourself to working with whole pieces of shells. You can crush eggshells and small clam shells to make a material which is particularly suited for filling in odd-shaped areas and creating a gravel-like texture. Also, consider using the glossy, pearly inside of mussel or oyster shells in some part of your picture.

Don't worry if other people call you a garbage collector. Remember that most artists are usually misunderstood.

VEGETARIAN MOSAICS

a unique collage using a mosaic technique

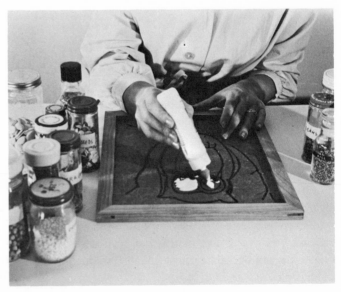

THIS PROJECT is one of the most exciting to do, for you'll be learning an unusual technique besides adventuring with texture and color. Ordinary mosaics are made from clay or glass tiles, called tesserae. In making Vegetarian Mosaics, however, *foodstuffs* and *spices* take the place of the tiles.

You will need these basic materials to begin: a piece of plywood for the background, or a *very* stiff piece of cardboard; white liquid glue; a pad of newspaper and clear lacquer for the final step of preserving your mosaic.

It would be impossible to list all the foodstuffs and spices that can be used to make a Vegetarian Mosaic, for such a list would run into hundreds of items. Your Vegetarian Mosaic will depend on what is available from your mother's kitchen or in nearby markets. The following is a partial listing of foodstuffs that I have

tried and found work well: pea, lima, fava, turtle, mung, kidney, pinto and coffee beans; tea, rosemary, laurel, oregano and mint leaves; curry, mustard and garlic powders; salt; pepper; instant and ground coffee; sesame, cumin, coriander, dill and poppy seeds; dried corn, peas and okra, rice; barley; cereals and many types of macaroni.

The first step is to draw your subject on the plywood background. If possible, put a frame on the plywood at this starting point. The frame acts as a "retaining wall" during the making of your Vegetarian Mosaic; it helps to keep the glue and foodstuffs in place. Study your available supply of tesserae, namely, the foodstuffs, deciding what material will be used for what area. Plan you mosaic for contrasts of color, texture and size of materials. I try to avoid outlining my subject with

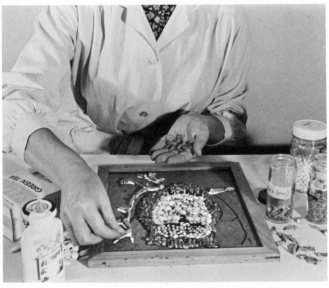

dark or light beans for this can make a hard and unattractive line.

Squeeze out enough glue to cover a small area of your subject. Select a foodstuff, perhaps kidney beans, and place it into the glue, fitting them carefully next to one another. Then work another area, applying more glue and filling that area with the chosen foodstuff.

You will notice that, before it dries, the white glue shows *between* pieces of foodstuff, such as between the beans. When this small area dries, the glue shows as an unattractive blank spot. Therefore, all such in-between areas must also be filled in by sprinkling a fine seed or powder, such as poppy or curry, over the *entire* large area in which the small spaces that exist. Press this fine material into the glue with your hand. The "fill" will

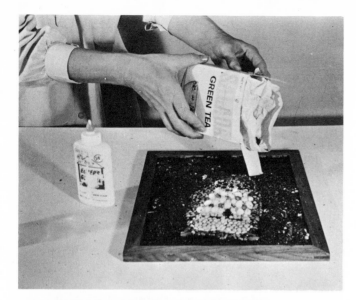

stay only where the glue is. When you wish to remove the excess material, lift the panel upright *quickly* and shake the "fill" onto a pad of newspaper. Since the glue is still wet, you must work very fast as you tip the panel or the glue and foodstuffs will slide from the plywood. Any excess materials collected on the newspaper can be poured into a bottle or box for later reuse. Continue to squeeze glue, place materials, fill in and remove excesses until the mosaic is completed, with the *exception* of the background.

For the background, choose your material carefully. You need a foodstuff that will be good for covering a large area and one that will, at the same time, contrast well with the materials used for your subject. I have found that products such as salt, poppy seed, ground

coffee or tea leaves are excellent for filling in large areas. Coat the entire background with glue, shake on the selected material and press it well into the glue. Allow your mosaic to dry for several hours or overnight before removing the excess of this last foodstuff.

Although a Vegetarian Mosaic will last a long time without a protective coat of lacquer, it is preferable to try to "seal" it against the ravages of time and insects. To do this, you must first allow your completed mosaic to dry out for a full week. Then apply two generous coats (allow drying time between coats) of clear lacquer. You'll be amazed to see how the lacquer brightens up the colors of the foodstuffs and, at the same time, adds the protection needed to insure a mosaic of long-lasting quality.

PLACTIC CUP CUT-UP

a wall hanging assembled from plastic rings

THIS DECORATIVE WALL HANGING is made by assembling slices cut from thermal beverage cups.

In this project you'll use the kind of thick-walled plastic hot beverage cup which is made from Styrofoam. You can substitute another type of cup, but the final result will differ from the sculpture illustrated in the photographs. This Styrofoam cup is usually sold bagged in large quantities and is quite inexpensive. You will also need sandpaper, rubber cement, a knife and metallic spray paint for the cups.

Begin by slicing ten to fourteen cups into rings, using an ordinary table knife. Vary the width of the rings from ½″ to 2″. Cut across some of the rings to produce half circles. If the edges of the slices are rough from cutting, smooth them with sandpaper.

Spread out all the pieces in front of you. Play with different combinations and groupings of shapes. Try nestling pieces within pieces. Place some rings at angles to one another. Add some of the solid-bottom circles, from the bottoms of the cups, here and there. Assemble small groups first, rather than trying to put together one large piece of sculpture. Later on, these small groups will be permanently connected into a single arrangement.

Rubber cement is one of the best glues to adhere the rings together. Other glues may dissolve the plastic material. When you are ready to glue, it is not necessary to take your groupings apart. Simply separate two touching pieces, brush on some rubber cement and press the two pieces back together as they were.

After experimenting with several arrangements, glue the smaller groups together to form the final large shape.

Allow the rubber cement to dry thoroughly. Your wall hanging can then be spray-painted to change it from its original white color. I like to use paint in metallic colors to give this feather-light plastic wall hanging the appearance of heavy brass or silver sculpture.

STRAW CONSTRUCTIONS

an assemblage of drinking straws

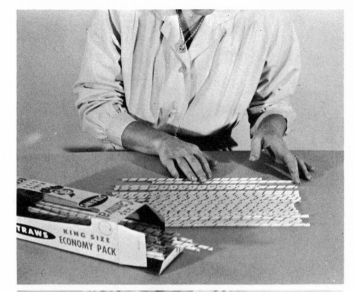

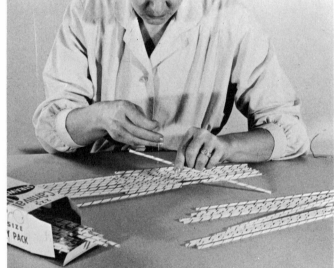

THIS PROJECT shows you how to string dozens of straws together to make a complex yet trim and linear construction.

The materials needed are a large box of paper straws either plain, patterned or transparent; a block of Styrofoam for the base; a slim dowel about two feet long and some very fine wire. (If you wish to paint your finished piece, you'll need spray paint in one or two colors. I like to use black plus a metal color.)

Snip a length of fine wire about 18″ long. If you can put this wire on a large needle, the threading will go quite quickly. Otherwise, you may find it necessary to puncture with a pin two tiny holes in each straw, about 1/3 the distance from one end, and then push the wire through. Thread this wire through one straw at a time.

Repeat this process until about forty to fifty straws have been threaded onto the wire. Stretch the wire out on your table, with the straws threaded onto it. Flip over every other straw so that half the straws have their long part on the left side of the wire and the other have their long part on the right side of the wire.

Now cut two shorter lengths of wire, about 7″ each. Using the same method, thread one of these wires through the loose ends of the straws on the left side and the other wire through the loose ends of the straws on the right side. Form a circle out of each of the three wires by twisting their ends together. When you do this the straws will take the shape of interlocking cones. You can help the shaping by spreading out the straws along the wire circles so that they are evenly spaced. This completes one section.

Assemble three or more of these sections. When you have done this, set the dowel upright into the Styrofoam base. This slender dowel (though nearly invisible in the finished piece) acts as the central support for the construction. Lower the first section onto the dowel so that the dowel passes between some straws but comes out through one of the smaller closed-circle ends. Lower a second section onto the dowel so that it is at any angle to the first section. When the straws on two sections meet, they will interlock with one another. Add the remaining sections by this threading-on and interlocking method.

Unless you've used colorful, transparent cellophane straws, you'll probably want to change the color of your finished construction. This is easily done with spray paint.

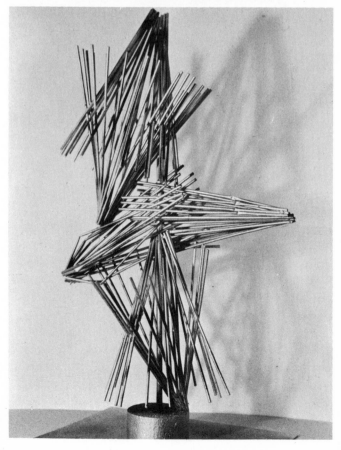

KITCHEN CLAY

a modeling material made on the stove

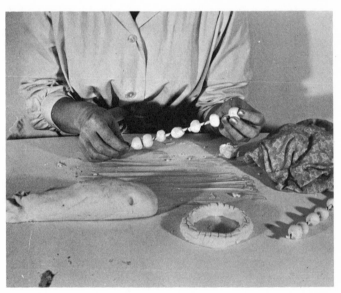

AN EXCELLENT, inexpensive modeling material can be made from a simple formula using a few ingredients from the kitchen. Kitchen Clay hardens without baking, and it can be easily modeled and then painted. The ingredients needed are baking soda, cornstarch and water.

Here's the "recipe": combine 4 cups of baking soda, 2 cups of cornstarch and 2½ cups of water in a saucepan. Warm this mixture over moderate heat, stirring constantly. When the mixture thickens to a dough-like consistency, turn it out onto a dish or sheet of tinfoil. When it is cool enough to handle, knead it for two or three minutes until it feels smooth.

Always cover Kitchen Clay with a damp cloth to keep it soft. If you want to keep it soft overnight, place it in a plastic bag and seal the bag tightly.

Kitchen Clay is modeled like any ordinary clay. It can be squeezed, rolled or pinched. You can make jewelry or you can make sculpture with it. You will find, however, that very large pieces develop cracks as they dry, so it is better to keep your pieces no larger than a big banana.

Perhaps you would like to make someone a string of beads for a present? To make a Kitchen Clay necklace roll out about twenty or thirty small balls. Thread these balls onto a few paper straws. The straws make a

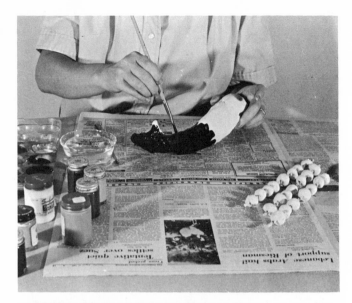

hole for stringing and also serve as a good holder for the beads while they harden and while they are being painted.

A bracelet can be made from the same kind of beads or, more simply, from a string of clay with its ends pinched together to form a circle.

You can even decorate the surface of the clay on whatever object you model by using any tool, flat or pointed. For example, a pencil point can be used to dent an interesting decoration into the soft clay.

Kitchen Clay will air-harden in one or two days. If the drying must be hurried, you can put your pieces in an oven which has been set at its lowest temperature for about three hours.

The dried clay is fairly hard and durable. It takes any kind of paint well, from poster to house paint. If you finish your poster-painted pieces with a coat of lacquer, this will enhance the colors, especially on painted beads.

To string your necklace, find a long length of heavy yarn or a shoelace. Tie the first bead at one end of this strand. Then tie a knot after this bead and add a second bead. Tie another knot. The beads are strung so that a knot always separates them. This knotting method uses fewer beads and makes the necklace lighter. End the stringing with a loop just large enough to pass over the first bead so that the ends of your necklace are connected.

'GATOR SCULPTURE

food cartons become an animal sculpture

IN TODAY'S SUPERMARKETS, fruits, vegetables and eggs come packaged in sturdy and colorful cartons which stimulate the imagination. Their odd shapes suggest subjects far from their original purpose.

This 'Gator Sculpture uses a few egg cartons, three rectangular-shaped cartons, some large pieces of stiff cardboard, colored tissue paper, glue or staples, paint and scissors.

First of all, draw an outline of a large alligator, about three feet long, from its neck to its tail, on heavy cardboard. Omit the head for now because that's constructed later. Cut out this outline. Then draw and cut out two pairs of legs from another piece of cardboard. Be sure to make the rear legs longer and fatter than the front ones, because that's the way an alligator is built.

Attach the legs by gluing or stapling them into place on the body shape. Glue or staple the body shape over a rectangular carton. This carton shapes the 'Gator's belly and lifts your sculpture off the ground to give it a more natural look. Now bend the legs so that they touch the ground.

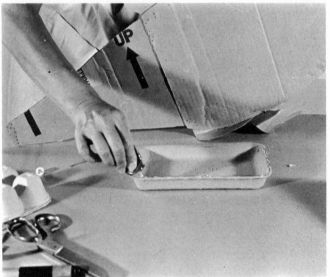

Glue several egg cartons to the back of the alligator, cutting and tapering them whenever necessary to fit the shape of the body. Be sure that some of the egg cups extend into the tail section.

To construct the head, staple or glue two same-sized rectangular cartons together at one end giving the appearance of gaping jaws. Taper the cartons and notch their edges to resemble snapping jaws with mean, jagged teeth.

Line the bottom and the roof of the 'Gator's mouth with crumpled, bright-pink tissue paper. Add halves of eggshells for its bulging eyes.

Join the head securely to the body by stapling or gluing these parts together.

Study a nature book in order to paint your 'Gator in a realistic way with green, black and brown. Use spray paint, if you can, for this will be easy. If you'd prefer to make a "fun" 'Gator, paint him in stripes, polka dots or checks!

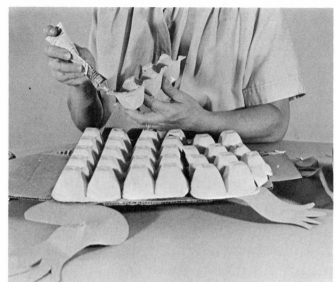

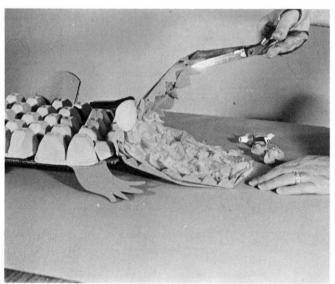

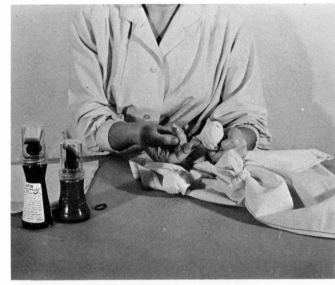

SHOE POLISH BANNER

tie-dyeing brought up to date

THIS PROJECT modernizes and simplifies a Victorian craft of fabric dyeing by using some of today's time-saving products. "Tie-dyeing" is the name given to this old yet new method of creating a design on fabric by bundling and tying the material so that the dye cannot by absorbed by all parts equally.

The materials needed to create your tie-dye banner are a large piece of white or pastel-colored cloth such as sheeting, elastic bands, paper towels, liquid shoe polish in 2 or more colors and 2 narrow dowels. Before actually dyeing, turn and stitch any ragged edges of your sheeting to give it "finished" look.

Begin by crumpling up a sheet of paper towel into a ball. Slip this ball under a part of the cloth and make a small lump by twisting the cloth around the paper ball. Hold the lump in place with a tight elastic band. Repeat this procedure, making many lumps scattered in a random pattern over the entire piece of cloth. However, be sure that the lumps are at least 6" apart.

Select one color of shoe polish. Wet the applicator

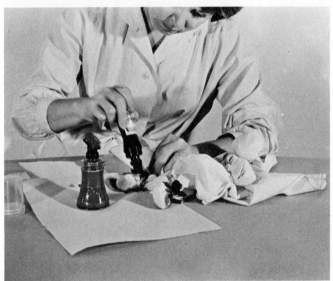

with polish and then dab the polish onto each of the lumps. Also apply the polish above and below the elastic bands. Don't try to drown the fabric with polish but let it go only where it flows by light dabbing. Change to a second color of polish and add touches of this color to the already-colored lumps.

Release all the elastic bands and discard the polish-stained wads of paper. Study the "accidental" design that you've made. Does your banner need more color? Is it patterned enough?

To complete the banner, tie some new lumps in un-dyed areas or overlap them with already-dyed spots. Experiment with different kinds of strokes and different amounts of polish. Release the bands once again and study your results. You'll probably agree that after

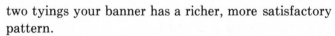

two tyings your banner has a richer, more satisfactory pattern.

When you have finished tying and dyeing, your banner will be quite wrinkled and in need of a pressing. After it has dried thoroughly, spread the banner flat on a thick pad of newspaper and iron it lightly with a medium-warm iron. You can expect that a little color will run from the cloth onto the paper.

Hang your banner by mounting it on the dowels. One dowel is placed along the top edge and the banner is glued or stapled to it. Tie on a length of cord or yarn across this dowel so that you can hang your banner. The second dowel, fastened to the bottom edge will weight the banner down. If a dowel isn't available any other straight sticks will do nearly as well.

"TAKE-AWAY" BLEACH PICTURES

a reverse painting venture

THE AIM OF THIS PROJECT is to *subtract* color rather than to add it. As a matter of fact, the color will disappear almost as fast as you "paint"! The materials needed are colored construction paper, a cupful of liquid bleach and a spoon, old brush, or paper straw for spreading the bleach.

Select a brightly-colored piece of construction paper, placing it in front of you on the table. Scoop up a little bleach with a spoon or on a brush. Drop the bleach

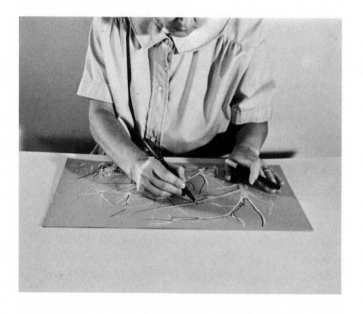 

onto your colored paper and *immediately* spread the blob around by brushing it or pushing it out with the spoon. Be careful of your clothes, because the color will fade them just as quickly as the paper.

For fun you can use a paper straw to blow at the drops of bleach. The force of your blowing will scatter the bleach in all directions, making long, fine lines. Within seconds, you will see the colored paper begin to fade and, in less than a minute, *all* the original color of the paper wet by the bleach will *disappear*. Delicate feathery lines, which look like twigs and grass, result from this technique.

If you've started with a fairly dark paper, the light, bleached lines will contrast sharply with it. If, however, your paper was of a lighter tone, you may want to add some dark, drawn lines for accent. Use ordinary crayons or a laundry marking pen to accent here and there.

DIP AND DAB

textured pictures printed with sponges

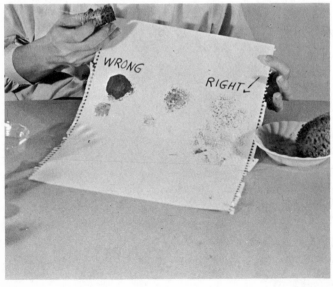

LOOK AROUND THE LAUNDRY for some sponges. You'll discover that sponges come in two types. Natural sponges which come from the ocean look rough with their large, irregular holes. Man-made sponges are usually smooth and regularly-shaped.

For materials you'll need a few pieces of sponge (either natural, man-made or both), poster paints, a jar of water, a shallow dish, scrap paper and paper for printing.

Pour a little paint into your dish. Dampen your sponge in water and squeeze it out well. Dip your sponge lightly into the paint. Dab the sponge on scrap paper until you can clearly see a print of the texture of your sponge. This texture print should have "holes" in it, somewhat like Swiss cheese. The holes will be either large or small depending on the type of sponge you are using.

Without dipping into the paint again, dab the sponge onto your good paper, making a clear print. Remember that printing is an up-and-down motion. Dragging your sponge will smear the print and make it fuzzy rather than crisp and clean.

When changing colors, rinse your sponge in clear water or use a separate piece of sponge for each color. If you print one color over another, be sure that the paint of the first print has dried or the colors will run together. "Draw" your picture. Build it sponge-print by sponge-print. If your picture needs some details or outlines, draw some lines with a laundry marking pen or with crayons.

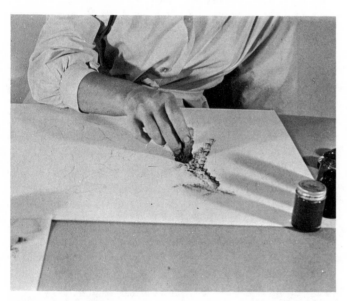
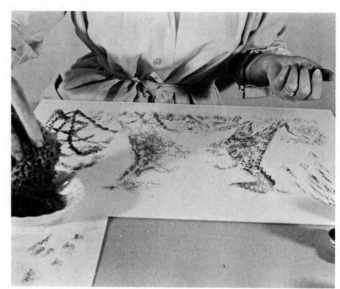

SOAP POWDER PICTURES

"printing" in relief

THIS PROJECT resembles a kind of "printing" although the method is rather unusual. A Soap Powder Picture starts with a piece of paper on which lines are "drawn" with a tube of glue. These wet glue lines are pressed into mounds of soap powder. When the different colored powders stick to the glue, the lines become visible and your picture emerges.

The materials needed are colored construction paper or ordinary cardboard, a tube of fast-drying glue, soap powder in one or two colors and a pencil.

If you investigate the housecleaning section of any supermarket, you'll find that laundry powders come in several colors in addition to the common white. Some powders are manufactured with green or blue dots scattered in the white powder, while other powders are all blue or all green. It's possible to "print" with a single color of powder, but your picture will be prettier if you can use two or three colors.

Pour out a small mound of each soap powder. Choose a background paper that contrasts with your soap powders. Sketch your subject on this background paper with a light pencil. Then retrace the lines with glue in a small section no more than a few inches wide. While the glue is still wet, flip your paper over quickly and press the glue into one of the soap powders. Lift the paper and tap it gently in order to remove the excess soap powder. The soap will stick only where there is glue. Continue to "print" your picture, section by section.

Colors are changed easily by dipping the wet glue lines into one color or another of soap powder. When the glue has dried, the raised-powder areas will be quite firm and hard.

Don't let your picture get wet. A Soap Powder Picture turns into a soap suds picture very easily!

YARN AND STARCH PICTURES

collages made without paste

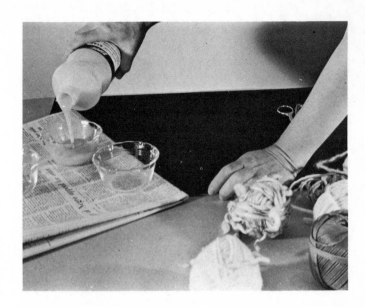

"COLLAGE" is the name given to artwork which is pasted or glued together. In this project, however, liquid starch takes the place of the "paste" and the pictures are "drawn" with yarn.

The materials you'll need are some small bowls, scissors, liquid starch, pieces of yarn and string and a stiff colored background. Your collage will be more attractive if you can find yarns of different colors and thicknesses, from fine fingering yarn to bulky rug yarn.

Pour a little liquid starch into the bowls. Snip some pieces of yarn into strands about 12" or so. Soak these strands in starch, separating the white yarn from the colored yarn in case some dye runs. Let the yarn absorb the starch for a few minutes. Then lift out a single strand. Remove the excess starch by running your fingers gently down the strand, allowing the excess starch to run back into the bowl. The yarn should look "wet," but starch should not be seen dripping from it.

Touch one end of a wet strand to your background paper, and with your fingers as guides, "draw" with the yarn as you drop it into place. Combine different colors and types of yarn as you "draw" your picture. Also, your collage will be more effective if you outline some areas and fill in other areas solidly.

It is difficult to keep your background clean and free from starch drips, no matter how carefully and neatly you work. A good many starch blobs can be avoided by not working with overly-wet strands of yarn and, of course, by not shifting any strands from one place to another, once it is part of your background.

When your Yarn and Starch Picture is finished, place it on some flat surface until it dries. Since its corners will tend to curl up a little as it dries, they must be weighted down without flattening any part of your picture.

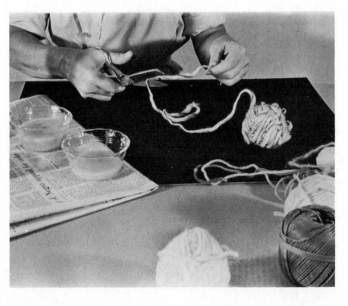

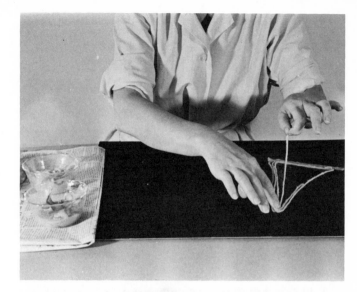

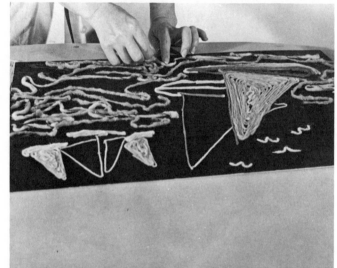

"TOUCH-ME" PLAQUES

a high-relief collage

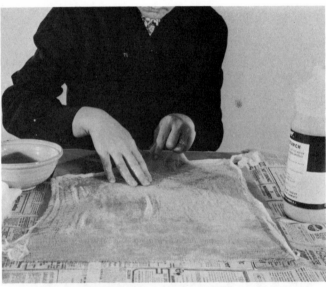

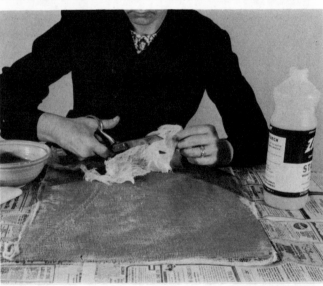

"TOUCH-ME" Plaques are collages made from ordinary cheesecloth and liquid starch. Their highly-raised surfaces invite your fingers to trace the designs and feel the texture. For materials you'll need cheesecloth, liquid starch, scissors, a bowl, stiff cardboard for a background and poster or spray paints.

Begin by cutting some cheesecloth into twenty or more strips about 1"–2" wide. Soak these strips in a bowl of liquid starch. Cut another piece of cheesecloth which is large enough to cover and wrap around your piece of cardboard. Dip this large piece of cheesecloth into starch and apply it directly to one side of the cardboard. Smooth the cloth until it is wrinkle-free and then turn the edges around to the back. Once the background is covered with cheesecloth, you can begin to shape your plaque.

With your subject in mind, place a strip of starch-soaked cheesecloth on the background and pull, push or pile it into the proper shape and position. Use your fingers to build up raised, rather than flattened, lines with the strips of cheesecloth.

Continue to build your plaque in this way, adding starch-soaked strips one by one, until it is completed. Then allow the plaque to dry overnight.

As it dries, the cardboard will probably begin to curl up in the corners. You can avoid this unpleasant happening by weighting the plaque down on all four corners while it is still wet. Be careful not to flatten any of its raised part as you apply the weights.

You'll notice that your dried plaque has taken on a faint blue cast—the color of the liquid starch. If you like this effect, you can consider your project finished. If you prefer to brighten the plaque you can paint it with poster paints or spray-paint it. Try adding a touch of gold or silver paint here and there for an interesting highlight.

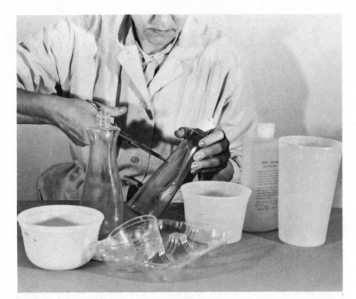

POPPING OUT PLASTER PARTS

casting in plastic molds

MANY LAUNDRY PRODUCTS (soap, bleach, starch, softener, detergent) come in plastic containers which have unique and interesting shapes. In this project, you will pour a mixture into several of these plastic containers to create plaster pieces which will later be combined into a single, exciting assemblage.

For materials you'll need several plastic containers in various shapes and sizes, sandpaper, water and plaster of paris. Begin by studying the shapes of your plastic containers. Since the container is your mold for future plaster shapes, you can fill it to any height that will give you a beautifully-cast shape. Can you get a better shape filling it partway or all the way to the top? It's up to you to decide how much plaster to pour into each container.

When you are ready to pour, mix the plaster according to directions but add more water than called for. A more liquid mixture takes longer to harden, and therefore, it will not begin to "set up" while you are in the midst of the delicate operation of pouring plaster into many molds! Fill at least five containers with plaster to the height you desire. A funnel will come in handy if you are guiding plaster into narrow-necked containers.

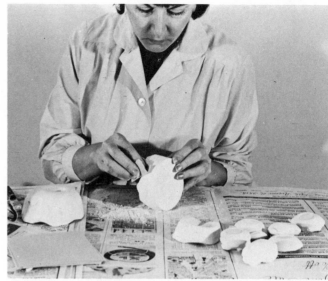

Leave the plaster in the molds until it dries. Then, free the plaster shapes from the molds. Usually, the shapes can be removed easily by "popping" them out as if they were ice cubes being released from a tray. However, if the shape of the mold is such that it imprisons your plaster piece, you must slit it open to release the casting.

When the shapes are removed from the molds, some of their edges might need sandpapering to smooth them out. If you like the white color of plaster, it is not necessary to paint your work. Otherwise, you can tone the shapes with almost any kind of paint, stain or varnish.

Place all the cast shapes before you on a table. Study them to see how they differ from one another. Begin to stack some shapes, experimenting with different arrangements. Your assemblage will be most effective if you do not pile up the shapes tightly, like bricks in a wall. Try some shapes at angles to one another. Overlap or overhang other pieces. Your assemblage is finished when the shapes you have grouped together please you. If you wish to keep this composition together permanently, you can attach touching pieces with a strong glue.

PLASTIC MAIDEN

a colorful, 3-dimensional plastic assemblage

TODAY many of our necessary and useful household products come in bottles, boxes and other containers formed from molded plastic. And the colors used in these containers are like a rainbow, from red to lavender! You can find blue, green, red, aqua, white and purple bottles holding laundry products, plus pink, yellow or turquoise containing scouring products. In the kitchen you'll find citrus juices dispensed in lemon and lime containers. Even the bottle caps are apt to be some bright color like orange or magenta. Once you've begun to search and collect these items, you'll be amazed at the variety of colors to be found.

The materials you'll need for the Plastic Maiden are plastic containers in many sizes, shapes and colors, a stiff background painted a dark color, scissors and glue.

Spread out your collection of plastic pieces and begin to arrange them on your background. Move the pieces around until they suggest the idea for your plastic assemblage. When you have your idea, you'll probably want to cut and shape some of the whole, rounded containers so that their edges will lie flat, for gluing, against the background. The cutting of plastic may be easy or difficult, depending on the thickness of that particular container. Avoid the tops and bottoms of bottles because they are molded from a double thickness of plastic and are nearly impossible to cut.

When you are completely satisfied with your arrangement of plastic pieces, you can begin to glue them permanently to your background. Lift each piece, one by one, and squeeze glue along its edges. Replace the piece into your assemblage. Experiment with different effects such as gluing plastic on top of plastic or clear plastic over colored plastic.

Your friends will enjoy trying to identify the products which gave you all the pretty colors in your assemblage.

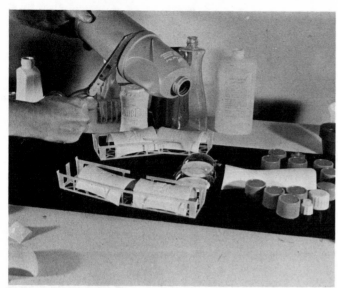

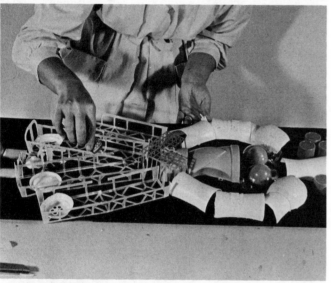

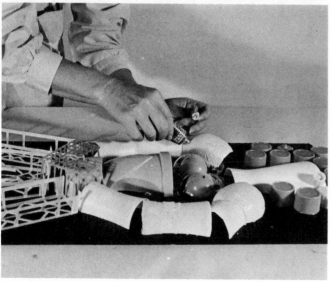

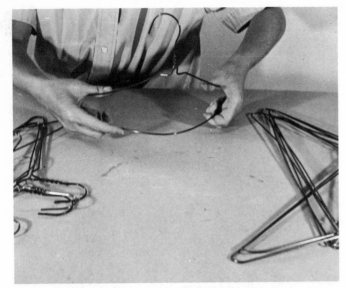

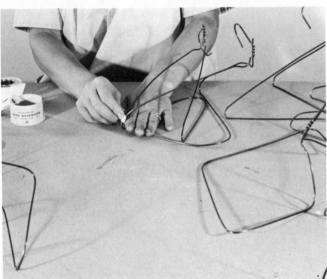

bending wire clothes hangers into new forms

NO MATTER how often you sort through your closets, almost every home ends up with too many wire clothes hangers. Here's an idea that uses up those extra hangers by bending them and combining them to make a piece of sculpture. This project is planned so that your hangers can be shaped by bending them, rather than requiring you to cut them into pieces, for cutting wire hangers is a difficult task.

The materials you'll need are 15–20 wire hangers, adhesive tape, liquid starch, paper towels, string and spray paints in one or two colors.

First, bend all your hangers in this way: hold a single hanger so that you are grasping the ends with both hands. Fold these ends toward each other so that they are then an inch or so apart. Bend the curved hanging hook so that it tips down to one side or the other. Shape half of your hangers into this #1 position. Shape the remaining hangers by pulling down on the bottom wire so that they assume a diamond-like shape. These two basic shapes are all that are necessary to build your sculpture.

Choose one bent-wire hanger of the first shape to serve as the sturdy base of your sculpture. Add a second hanger, of either shape, to this base hanger, intertwining the wires as much as possible. Hold these two hangers in place by using narrow strips of adhesive tape to join the points where the wires of each hanger touch one another.

Your sculpture is built hanger-by-hanger. Always secure each additional hanger to an earlier one by means of strips of adhesive tape. Whenever you add a new hanger, tilt it so that the curved hook falls within the sculpture, near its center. Build your piece upward and outward until it takes on a balanced and likable shape. At this early stage, your sculpture will look like a wire skeleton!

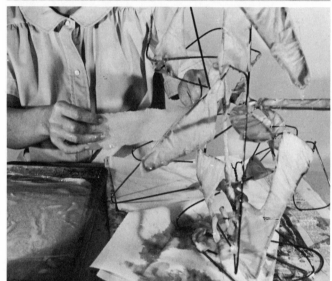

Next, tear sheets of paper towels into strips about 6″ wide. Soak them in liquid starch, keeping them as flat as possible. (A cookie tin is ideal for immersing them.) Lift out a single strip and run your fingers down it to remove the excess starch. Stretch this strip between two sections of wire and wrap the leftover ends around the wire to secure them. Continue to stretch strips between many wires, but do not cover them completely. To keep an open look to your sculpture you can add some pieces of string, dipped in starch, and wind them throughout the piece.

Your finished sculpture should have a light and airy look, rather than a heavy, closed look. Place your completed sculpture on a thick pad of newspaper to catch all the starch that will drip as it dries.

Your Hanger-Up Sculpture can be painted with ordinary poster or house paints, but spray paints are easier to use for their fine spray of color covers all those inner, hard-to-reach spots. If you like the look of welded metal, spray your piece with a combination of black paint and highlight it with gold or copper paint.

MASKS FROM BALLOONS

shape two masks at one time

IT'S ALWAYS a good idea to know how to construct a mask, for this knowledge often comes in handy. There are times when you might need a mask for Halloween or to portray a character in your school play. Perhaps you'd like to make a mask just to decorate a wall in your room.

This project describes how to make two masks at one time. You can use both masks for yourself, or you can share one with a friend. For materials you'll need a large oval-shaped balloon, newspaper, paper towels, liquid starch, a bowl, rubber bands, scissors and paints.

First, blow up your balloon to face size. Fasten the end closed with a rubber band. Then cut or tear newspaper into strips about 1″–2″ wide. Allow these strips to soften in liquid starch for at least ten minutes. Pick out a single strip of newspaper and paste it to your balloon. Add more of these strips, one by one, pasting them in the same direction as the first strip, until the balloon is covered.

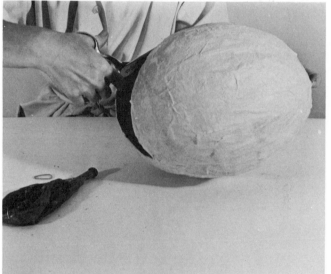

Paste on three more layers of newspaper, strip by strip. Each time you add a new layer, change the direction of the strips. This gives your mask maximum strength. After you build up four newspaper layers, add two more made from strips of paper towels. These final two layers will give you a smooth finish for the painting step which comes later.

Allow this six-layered balloon to dry for at least two or three days. When it feels dry, release the rubber band and the shriveled balloon will drop out. Then pencil a line around the starched shell form to divide it into equal halves. Cut along this guide line with scissors. You'll now have two identical oval shapes, each of which can become a mask. It's up to you to fashion a "personality" for your mask. Will you create an imaginary creature or will you make a famous person? Will your mask be fierce or will it be angelic? When you've decided on your "personality," you can shape the features with narrow strips of starch-soaked paper towels. Build up eyes, noses, horns, teeth, lips, ears, hair or hats . . . it's up to you! Allow the masks to dry once more, and then paint them with poster paints or house enamels.

The final steps are to cut slits for seeing through the eyes and puncturing tiny holes, at the earline, to attach strings for holding the mask on.

Tired of being the same old self? Then put on a mask and be someone else!

MULTIPLES

abstract designs traced from outline

INTERESTING ABSTRACT PICTURES can be created by tracing different outline forms and interweaving and overlapping them into different arrangements. And what is a better source for such outlining forms than your attic?

First of all, collect several small objects that can be easily traced around, such as a knife, fork, spoon and a bell, or puzzle pieces, nutcrackers and scissors. You'll also need drawing paper and some crayons or colored felt-tipped pens.

Select an object and place it anywhere on your drawing paper. Trace around it making an outline. Move the object to a new spot; place it at a different angle than before and trace around it once more. Choose other objects, tracing around them and overlapping their outlines with those drawn earlier. Change their position on your paper as much as possible. Continue to outline different objects until your paper is full of tracings from edge to edge.

The next step is to create patterns within these traced outlines. For this step, you can use paints, crayons, colored pencils or felt-tipped pens. I like to draw with felt pens for their narrow pen point allows me to include many small details. Now draw patterns within each section of your outline. Draw stripes, checks, solids, polka dots or design some never-been-seen-before patterns of your very own. Be sure not to repeat the same pattern in two neighboring areas. Your design will probably look more organized if you limit your choice of colors to a few instead of using a rainbow-like assortment. Your finished abstract design will be vibrant with pattern and color.

If you think it is fun to make an abstract design using many different object-outlines in one picture, do you think it would be as much fun if you limited yourself to only one or two objects? It's just as much fun. Try it!

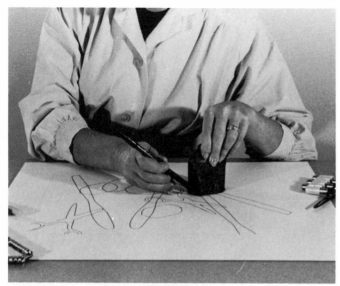

SGRAFFITO

a drawing, painting and etching technique

SGRAFFITO IS THE NAME given to an etching technique that uses a pointed tool to scratch through a covered surface to reveal another surface below. This project describes how to apply a thick layer of wax crayons onto a background which is then covered over with a coat of thick, dark paint. Then a pointed tool is used to scratch through that dark surface revealing the bright colors of the coat underneath.

For materials you'll need wax crayons, dark poster paint (or India ink), a pointed tool for etching and a stiff material such as a floor tile or piece of cardboard for the background.

Begin by coloring your background with irregularly-shaped areas of bright colors, using wax crayons. As you color, bear down hard on your crayons so as to leave behind a thick layer of wax. Fill in your background completely until no uncolored speck can be seen.

The next step is to coat the entire crayoned surface with poster paint or India ink, in your darkest color. You can also use dark wax crayons but I've found that the best results are obtained from paint or ink. As you apply the dark paint, the color should disappear completely. If you can still see color through the dark paint, your surface needs a second coat. Wait for the paint or ink to dry and then go on to the next step.

Select a pointed tool for etching your Sgraffito. This tool can be a knitting needle, a toothpick, a hatpin or a long nail. You'll soon discover that almost any slightly-pointed instrument will scratch through the paint layer to reveal the layer of color underneath. Experiment with different tools to see what kinds of lines they create. Draw your picture directly on the paint with one of these tools, using fine and broad strokes.

As you work along be sure to etch just deep enough to penetrate the dark layer. Be careful that you do not dig deeper into the background material itself.

When you try Sgraffito the next time, why not limit your crayons colors to two or three instead of working with many colors? Try it. You'll like the results!

STAMP PAD STAMPINGS

a simple method of relief printing

STAMP PAD STAMPINGS is a kind of relief printing that is fun and simple to do. Once you've tried it, you'll learn that it is good for picture-making and for designing other things such as greeting cards and wrapping paper.

The materials you'll need are one or two inked stamp pads (black plus one other color is good) and hard objects for printing such as a key, can opener, plastic bottles, bits of hardware, hair curlers and even your own fingertips! You'll also need paper to print on, some newspaper and some paper towels for cleanup.

Place your printing paper on some flat surface, such as a table, and then slip a thick pad of newspaper under it. This newspaper will help make your printing surface "bouncier" and thus better for printing than a hard, unbending surface.

Select one of your printing objects. Press this object into the ink-moistened stamp pad, rolling it slightly from side to side to ink it completely. Press this inked object to your paper, again rolling it from side to side in order to make a complete impression of its inked surface. Make a second print before you reink the object.

Experiment with all your objects and try different ways to create patterns. What sort of a pattern do you get from printing one object-print over another object-print? What happens when you print one color over another? Explore all the ways of combining prints and colors to create original, exciting patterns.

When you are finished printing, be sure to wipe the ink from all the objects that you've used with paper towels.

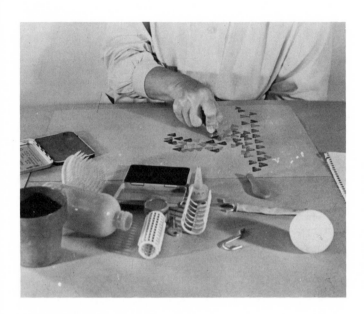

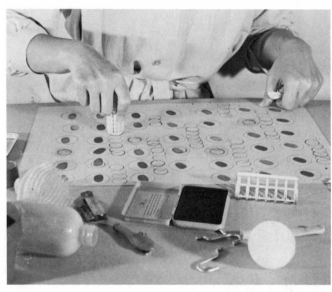

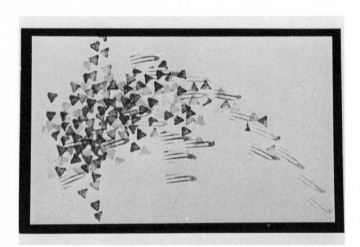

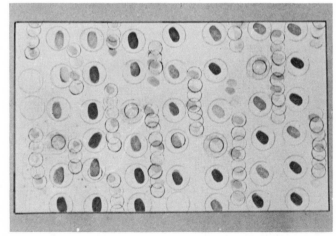

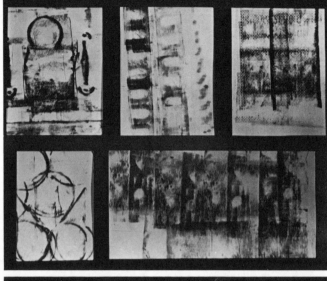

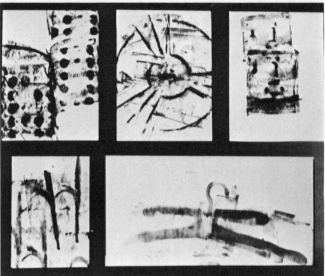

ATTIC PRINTS

relief printing from found surfaces

THIS EXCITING PRINTING PROJECT shows you how an inked brayer (a roller for printing) and some paper can record all kinds of unusual textures that can be found in your attic or in any other storage area. In this method of printing, you'll roll an inked brayer over a textured surface that has been covered with a sheet of paper. The ink transfers an impression of that covered-up surface to paper, making it visible. Once you've tried this simple method, you'll want to search all over your house for textures interesting enough to record on paper.

For materials you'll need a brayer, printing ink and paper.

To start, find some very rough surface such as a straw basket or an old, wooden ceiling beam. Place a piece of paper over this surface and hold it in place with one hand as you roll your inked brayer back and forth over it.

You'll see an impression of that covered-up surface appear immediately! Then try a print of the hinges on an old steamer trunk. Compare that print with a lock print from a more modern suitcase. Make a print of the brass andirons tucked away in some far corner or try a print taken from some wooden hangers. "Print" the wire basket on an electric fan or experiment with a print taken from the carved edge of a piece of furniture.

You'll want to assure your mother that, although you are working with printer's ink, you are not soiling anything. Remind her that a sheet of paper always lies between your inky brayer and the object that you are printing from.

There's no limit to the number and variety of prints that you can make in this way. Try making a print of everything in sight.

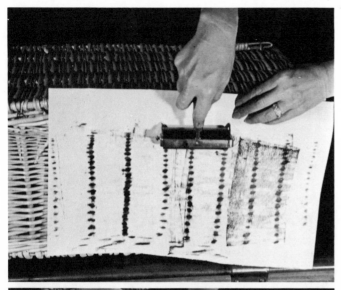

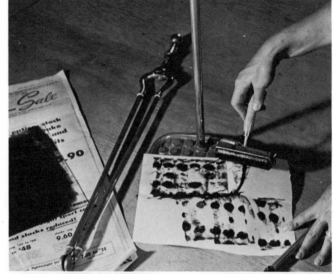

TEAR AND TELL

pictures torn from newspaper

DID YOU EVER want to make a picture only to discover that you were out of paint and crayons? And, to make things worse, you couldn't even locate some scissors and construction paper. Don't dismay! You can still make a wonderful picture if you can find some newspaper, paste, and a piece of dark paper for the background.

First, turn to the classified section of the newspaper. This section is used in Tear and Tell pictures, for its long columns and photoless pages make it ideal for this project. Think about, and decide upon, a subject for your picture. Then, with some part of your picture in mind, tear a shape from the newspaper. Use your nimble fingers to tear the paper so that it becomes a person, a table, a boat or whatever your particular picture needs. Imagine! You've made your fingers become a pair of scissors! Tear, tear, tear many pieces, until your picture is completed.

Then arrange these torn, shaped pieces on your dark background. Move them around until you think they are in the right position to tell your story. Then you can paste these pieces to the background. Use just enough paste to stick them; too much paste will only ooze out at the edges.

Not all your pieces need be pasted flat. You can build up texture in your picture in several ways. For example, you can paste pieces of newspaper on top of other pieces to create a thickness or you can curl, pleat or fold pieces of newspaper. Keep your background plain and simple, for the newspaper will show up more effectively against an uncluttered background.

And there it is—a picture made from practically "nothing"!

HODGEPODGE COLLAGE

a composition made from odds and ends

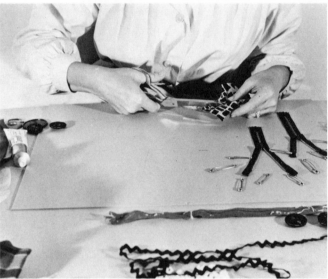

AN ARRANGEMENT of things that are pasted together is called a collage. When that arrangement is whimsically put together from odds and ends, I call it a Hodgepodge Collage. Using odds and ends for picture-making will open your eyes to the beauty and usefulness of things which so often end up in the wastebasket. It's also fun to take an everyday item and give it a witty new "life." For example, the zipper on your jacket has the job of holding the two sides closed. In a Hodgepodge Collage, however, a zipper could become the trunk of a tall tree, or the steel of train tracks or even the spindly legs of a skeleton. Everything that you find and collect can take on another useful personality in a collage.

Before you can start your picture-making, you must first stock up with a collection of "things." (There's no limit to the kinds and amounts of things that you can gather, once you get started!) Try to include some of the following: bits of yarn, odd-shaped buttons, broken zippers, scraps of fabric, knitting needles, plastic bobbins, greeting cards, theater programs, paper doilies, game parts, gummed stickers, ribbons, Christmas trim, ends of wallpaper, string or pieces of leather. You'll also need a piece of paper or cardboard for the background and glue. Once you have some (or all) of these "things," you can begin to experiment with subject ideas.

Select some objects at random and arrange them on your background. Move them around or exchange them for other things until an idea for a picture is suggested to you. Rearrange and change things until your arrangement of objects satisfies you. Always try for the greatest variety of thicknesses, color and texture in every picture that you make. Contrast smooth paper with rough leather, or use flat, delicate lace next to thick, wooden puzzle parts. Glue this arrangement of objects to your background.

Sometimes the idea of a story-telling collage can be made clearer by adding cutout figures of people or animals, taken from pages of old, discarded magazines. When these figures are in your collage, they often supply the necessary ingredient to help viewers understand what you are saying in your picture.

DIORAMAS

assembled from premolded shipping forms

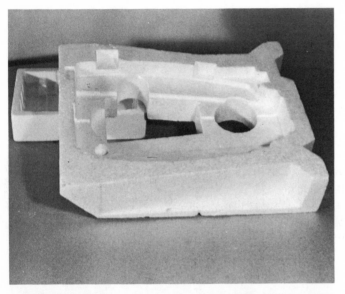

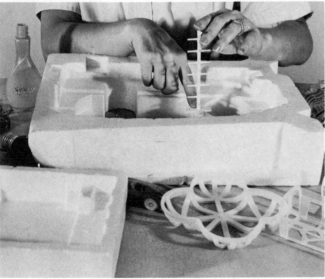

WHEN TELEVISION SETS, radios and cameras are packed for shipment, they often are held securely within their carton by a thick, foamy plastic material which has been molded around them. This shipping form is the stimulating basis for a Diorama.

First, you must locate one of these packing pieces. If you can't find one around your house, ask a friendly shopkeeper to save one for you. When you've found your shipping piece, study its shape well.

Stretch your imagination to turn this shipping piece into something new and unique. Could this plain white form become a lunar city? Or could it be shaped into a children's zoo? If you added racing cars and guardrails could it become a speedway? Once you've decided upon the theme for your Diorama, scout around for the right odds and ends that will turn it into the Diorama of your imagination.

All kinds of ordinary, everyday materials can become something different in a Diorama. For example, plastic containers for vegetables become fences and walls, and checkers or marbles pave streets. Sometimes small boxes become houses and stables and burnt-out flashbulbs become bushes. Every scrap you use is turned into something new, in miniaturized form.

When you are constructing your Diorama, you can usually keep things in place by pressing part of them into the soft plastic material. Figures of people, animals and vehicles can be clipped from magazines and mounted on cardboard to add to your Diorama. You will want to glue some things in place permanently, but it will be much more fun if you leave things like cars and people unglued so that you can move them around your Diorama while you tell a story.

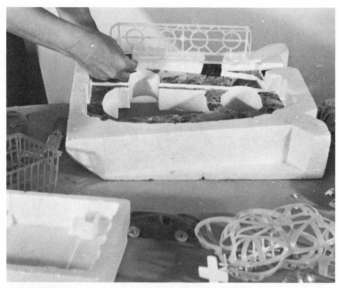

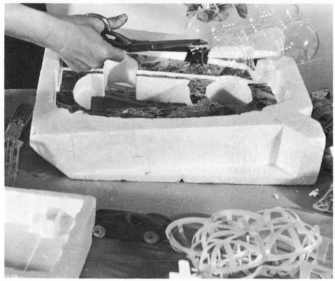

MOBILES IN ORBIT

moving sculpture assembled from magazine illustrations

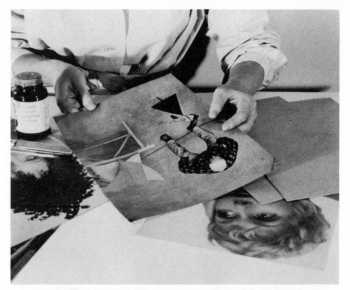

THIS MOBILE IN ORBIT "floats" in the air, and even in the faintest breeze, its shapes-within-shapes turn and twist actively. It starts from a single sheet of cardboard which has been covered on both sides with illustrations clipped from magazines. The cardboard is cut apart and reassembled to produce ever-changing forms and pictures.

For materials you'll need a sheet of cardboard for each mobile (the illustrations show two mobiles; one is rectangular, the other circular), colored paper or full-page illustrations from magazines, scissors, ruler or compass, paste and a needle with thread.

Begin by covering both sides of the cardboard in one of the following ways:

—paste full-page magazine illustrations on both sides, or

—paste plain paper on one side, patterned paper on the reverse side or

—paste light paper on one side, dark paper on the reverse side.

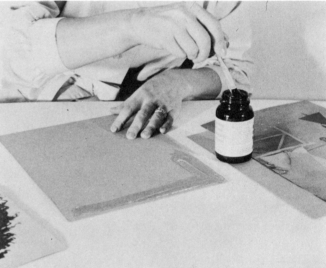

Then choose one of these basic shapes for your mobile —a rectangle, a square, a circle or a diamond. Draw this shape (with compass or ruler as needed) as large as will fit onto your covered cardboard. This will be the outline of your finished mobile.

Mark the center point of this outline. Now draw a smaller outline on the cardboard, 1½" closer to the center. Repeat this reducing-and-drawing, making each outline about 1½" smaller than the one before. The smallest shape probably should not be less than 2"–3" across. You will need a total of three, four or five shapes-within-shapes.

Now cut out the outlines you have drawn. Then trim ¼" from the outside edge of all the pieces. This trimming step is very important in later achieving a mobile

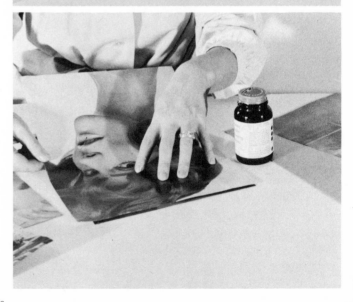

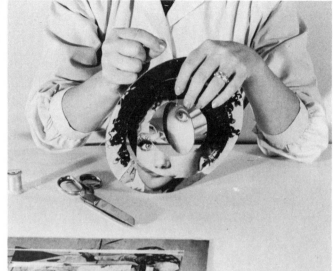

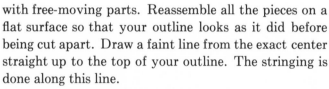

with free-moving parts. Reassemble all the pieces on a flat surface so that your outline looks as it did before being cut apart. Draw a faint line from the exact center straight up to the top of your outline. The stringing is done along this line.

In order to string your mobile together, you begin with the smallest, innermost piece and work out toward the largest piece. Thread a needle with a long thread, knotted at one end. Pass the needle through the top of the smallest piece, as close to the edge as possible, on your faint "stringing line." Pick up the second piece and pass the needle through it, as close to its lower edge as possible, on the "stringing line." Make a knot between the two pieces so that the first piece dangles freely. Pass the needle through the second piece, as close to its upper edge as possible, on the "stringing line." (Do not make a knot at this point; knots are used only to keep an upper piece from sliding down onto a lower piece.) Pick up the third piece and pass the needle through it as you did on the second piece. Continue to add the remaining pieces by string and knotting as before. After you've knotted the last piece in place, be sure to leave a length of thread for hanging.

Now hang up your mobile and study its turning motion. Does it move freely? If so, you need not make any adjustments. Do some pieces bump one another? If so, see if they have been trimmed enough or if they have been strung properly. Adjust the string or the trimming so that your mobile will move easily in the slightest breeze.

To begin, cut many pieces of wire into different lengths from 5″ to 16″ long. You'll need at least 15 pieces of wire. Bend each wire in the following shape: starting at the center, use pliers to bend a small loop which points upward. Then, at each end of the wire, bend loops that face downward. Don't bend the end loops to a closed position, for this is done as a later step. Bend all your wire pieces into this shape before you continue to the next step. A mobile of this type begins with its lowest wire to which are added other wires, working upward toward its highest wire at the hanging point. (Generally, the lowest wire is also the shortest wire.)

Remove any strings or clips which may be attached to the identification tags. Select one of the short wires; hang a tag on each end by threading it onto a partially open loop. Now close the loop with your pliers. Choose a second wire of a different length. This time connect one of its end loops to the center loop of the first wire. Close the loop that joins these two wires. Then add a tag to the empty end for balance and close that loop. Your mobile grows by this linking and balancing of wires and balance pieces.

There is a good deal of similarity between balancing a mobile and trying to balance on a seesaw with a friend who weighs more than you do. You can balance one another, even though your weights are not equal, if you shift your weight back and forth toward the center of the seesaw. Sometimes your mobile is quite balanced and then, as you increase its size, you add a wire with tags that makes it tilt. So you must balance it once more, by adding more weight to the other side.

In its early stages, while it is still small, you'll be able to hold your mobile in one hand as you work upon it with the other. But, as it grows larger and more complicated, it must be suspended so that you can work upon it and, at the same time, judge its balance and beauty.

The very best way to understand how to build and balance a bent-wire mobile is to make one yourself. Do try it. It's lots of fun!

TAG MOBILES

animated sculpture made from bent wire

THIS PROJECT describes how a mobile can be constructed from bent-wire pieces. Colored, round identification tags hang on the ends of the wires to balance the sculpture. Once you understand the principles of construction, assembly and balance, you can go on to create other such sculptures, substituting various materials in the place of the identification tags called for in this project.

The materials you'll need are medium-weight wire, pliers and colored identification tags.

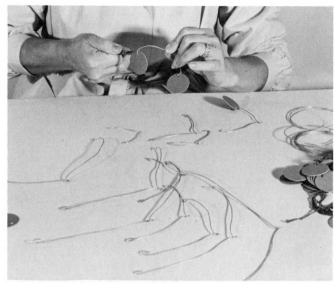

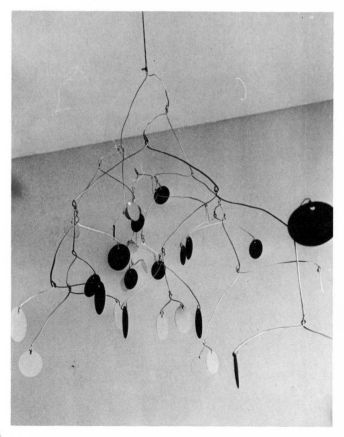

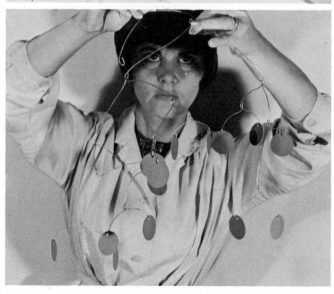

CIGAR HOLDER SCULPTURES

an experiment with fused plastics

IN ORDER TO CONSTRUCT a piece of sculpture like the one in the picture, you will have to know some cigar smokers. Then you'll have to find one among them who prefers cigars of the plastic-tipped variety. Ask your cigar smoker to save the next 30 or 40 plastic holders for you.

When you have amassed such a hoard, soak them overnight in soapy water in order to remove any remnants of tobacco left inside the tips. Drain, rinse and dry the holders. The rest of the materials can be gathered when the tips are drying.

For the base you'll need a block of wood or cork. You'll also need a short piece of stiff wire, kitchen tongs and a candle. When I experimented with different brands of cigar tips, I found that they are all non-flammable as they certainly ought to be! Even so, an

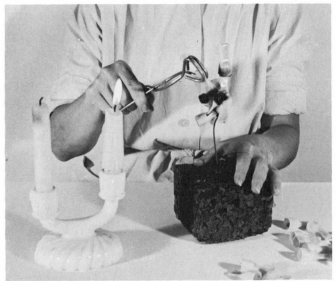

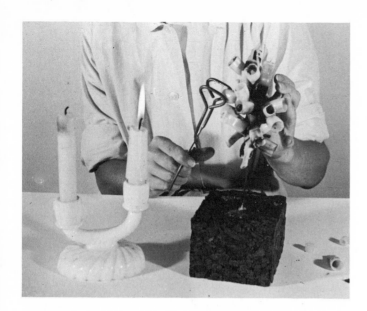

adult should always be present when you are working with a lighted candle. As an extra security measure, also use the tongs while melting and fusing the tips, to guard against possible mishaps and scorched fingers.

For assembling your structure, you can substitute strong glue instead of melting the tips in the candle flame if you prefer. However, if you glue your sculpture together, instead of fusing it, the pieces will remain uniformly cream-colored rather than develop the carbon black areas produced by the flame.

Begin the sculpture by inserting a short, stiff piece of wire into the wood or cork base. Bend the wire slightly at the tip. Thread the wire through the hole in the plastic tip; the bend in the wire holds the tip suspended from the base. It is upon this first tip that the rest of the sculpture will be built. Using tongs, pick up a second plastic tip. Hold either end of it in the candle flame. Keep it there until it appears to soften and begins to blacken. Press this warm, softened piece to the first tip, mounted on the wire. Hold the pieces together, for a moment, until they stick and fuse to one another.

Your sculpture grows in size by building it up piece by piece, that is tip by tip, steadily adding to its height and width. You can vary its shape by fusing the plastic tips at different angles, or you can even nestle small tips within larger ones.

Turn your sculpture as you work so that it will have balance and form when viewed from all sides. The final size and shape of your sculpture will be determined only by your own imagination and the number of tips with which you have to work.

PLASTIC BOX STENCILING

a dry brush technique

MANY ARTISTS like to work with their brushes fairly dripping with paint. But there is another perfectly good painting technique that starts with a brush that has very little paint on its bristles. This technique is called "dry brush" painting, and our project combines this with a stenciling technique to create unusual designs on paper from ordinary plastic fruit and vegetable containers with holes.

For this project you will need a few plastic fruit or vegetable containers, house paint or poster paint in one or two colors, a stiff straight-edged brush, newspaper and white or colored paper.

Before you begin to stencil, you must prepare your brush so that it has the proper amount of "dryness." First, dip the tip of your brush into paint lightly. Then work the brush back and forth on a thick pad of newspaper until most of the paint comes off. When you can see individual marks made by the hairs of the brush, you'll know that you've removed enough paint. Even though your brush is termed "dry," you'll be amazed to see how many designs you can stencil with the tiny amount of paint remaining within the bristles.

Choose one of the plastic boxes. Look at it and you'll discover that a single box contains several different designs. Usually the pattern on the ends of the box differs from the patterns on its sides and bottom. Place your box on white or colored paper and hold it in place with one hand. Then stab your almost-dry brush at the grillwork design of the plastic box with a vigorous, repeated, up-and-down motion. This stabbing action allows the paint to penetrate the paper while the grillwork of the plastic blocks out certain areas of that paper, creating a stenciled design. Lift the plastic container carefully and study this stenciled design.

Once you have mastered this simple technique, you can go on to explore further with design and color. Try stenciling one color over another or one design on top of another. Does your stencil change if you use a rough paper instead of a smoother paper? The excitement really begins when you begin to experiment with design, color and texture.

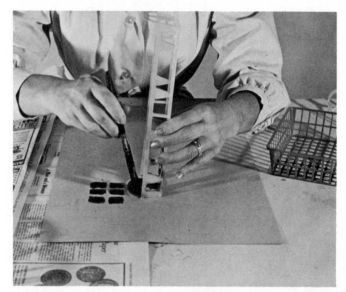

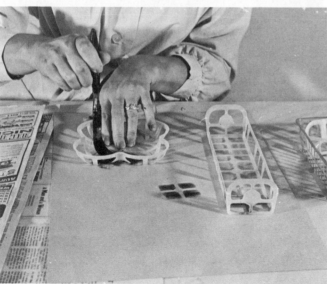

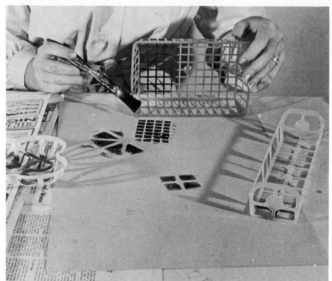

CORRUGATED PICTURES

painted optical illusions

THERE ARE some kinds of paintings that try to fool your eye, leading you to believe that a picture is moving, while it is not moving at all! There are many ways to achieve this optical illusion, most of which are quite complicated. This project shows you a simplified way to create an optical motion effect. And it goes one step further, in that this Corrugated Picture (which already makes your eye jump a little) has parts which actually do turn and move within the picture!

The materials needed are a large sheet of corrugated cardboard and a similar-sized sheet of smooth cardboard, some round objects, like cans or plates, a pencil, two colors of paint, scissors, paste and two or three paper fasteners.

First trace around your round objects, outlining several circles on the sheet of corrugated cardboard. While you are tracing the circles, overlap some of them. Then trace some square-edged shapes onto the same cardboard, overlapping them with some of the circles.

The next step is to prepare your paints, making a third, blended color from the original two colors. Take a small portion of each of the starting colors and mix them together. This mixing gives you three related colors.

Your ridged cardboard background has already been divided into geometrical shapes by tracing and overlapping circles and squares. Consider each divided part of every circle or square as a separate area. Each area will be painted in its own individual way, using only three colors in various combinations of solids and stripes. Let us assume that your three "colors" are black, white and gray. With these colors, and using the ridges of the corrugated as guidelines for stripe-making, you can pattern in the following ways: you can paint some areas all black, all white or all gray or you can paint black and white stripes, gray and white stripes or gray and black stripes.

To create the best optical effects, all touching areas must be a different solid or striped pattern. Painting a Corrugated Picture takes thought and time, but it is well worth the effort when you see bold designs emerge from this careful planning.

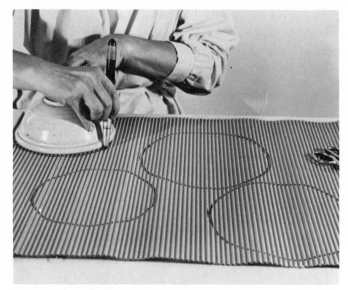

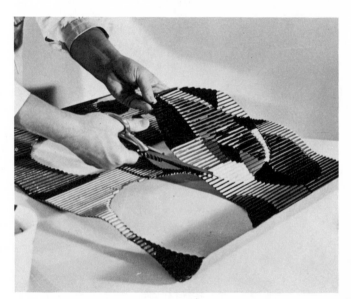

Allow the painted cardboard to dry thoroughly. Then cut out two or three whole circles from it. Paste the remaining sheet (from which the circles have been cut) to the smooth sheet of cardboard. Now, push paper fasteners through the centers of the cutout circles and fasten these circles back into place on the larger, painted cardboard. Touch up the brass heads of the paper fasteners with a dab of matching paint so that they blend in with their surroundings.

Your finished Corrugated Picture will be very "active"! You can make it "jump" a little more by turning some of the circles so that their stripes are at angles to other striped areas.

PRINTS FROM PLASTER

a printing technique

THIS PRINTING PROJECT starts with a thin slab of plaster which has been cast from a milk carton mold. Using plaster for your printing block is an excellent idea for it is inexpensive, it can be easily engraved and it lasts a long time.

For materials you will need plaster of paris, a cardboard milk carton in quart or half-gallon size, printing ink, a brayer (an ink roller), a pointed tool for etching, a sheet of cardboard for rolling out the ink, scrap paper and a pencil and colored or white paper for printing.

First, you must cast your printing block from plaster. Mix enough plaster to fill a milk carton to a thickness of 1½″ – 2″. Pour the plaster into the carton and allow it to harden overnight. When the plaster feels dry, tear off the cardboard carton. (The plaster will not stick to the plastic-coated inner lining of the carton.)

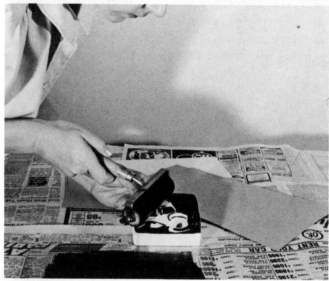

Plan a simple design or picture on scrap paper. Transfer this design to your plaster block by drawing it directly or by using carbon paper. Then use a pointed tool (a long nail or screwdriver) to engrave your picture or design into the soft plaster along these drawn lines. Coat your brayer with ink and roll this brayer over the engraved plaster block. Vary your direction of rolling ink so that the block is totally covered with an even application.

Place a sheet of paper on top of the ink and rub your palm over the paper in a circular motion. This kind of rubbing motion is called burnishing and transfers the ink from your printing block to your paper to create a print. Peel off the paper slowly and examine your first print. You may have "pulled" a perfect print on your first try but, more likely, your first prints will not be your best prints. It takes a little experimenting before you know how much to ink a block and how much to burnish a print.

To make more prints simply reink your block. Keep "pulling" prints until you get several good ones. A single block of plaster lasts a very long time before it starts to wear out. If you want to, you can make two hundred or more prints from one block before it begins to crumble. You can see why it is an excellent way to make posters and greeting cards!

WEATHER STRIPPING PRINTS

impressions from felt strips

HERE'S AN INEXPENSIVE and readily-found material that needs little preparation to be made into an excellent printing substance. When this thick felt material is glued to a background and inked thoroughly, its highly-raised surface makes an ideal relief-type printing plate.

For this project you'll need a few feet of weather stripping, glue, scissors, stiff cardboard, household paints (or printing ink), a brayer (an ink roller) and paper for printing.

First, decide whether you will make an abstract design print or a print with a realistic theme. An abstract design is created easily by snipping a length of weather stripping into small, geometrical shapes such as rectangles, triangles, diamonds or squares. These shapes are arranged and glued onto a sheet of stiff cardboard, forming a pleasing abstract design.

A realistic picture starts from an outline of your subject drawn on stiff cardboard. (Keep it simple and work as large as possible.) The weather stripping is then cut into strips to fit the contours of your outline. Next, these pieces are glued securely to the cardboard to create the printing plate.

Spoon out some household paint (or squeeze out some printing ink) onto a thick piece of cardboard. Roll the brayer back and forth in the paint until it is well "inked." Then roll this brayer over the felt weather

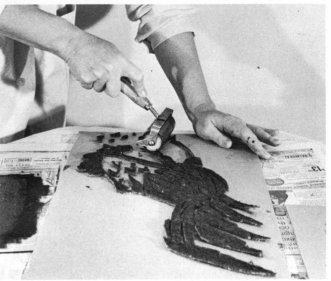

stripping printing plate. When you do this, only the felt receives the ink because it is raised higher than the cardboard on which it is mounted. This method of printing is known as relief printing.

Place a sheet of paper over the inked surface. Rub the paper hard with the palm of your hand, making a circular motion. Peel off the paper slowly and examine your first print. Usually the first few prints will be uneven until the weather stripping becomes thoroughly "seasoned" (inked). Reink your plate and try other prints until you "pull" a perfect one.

This method of printing is good for making a single print or dozens of prints. Even the used, once-inked weather stripping plates are attractive enough to frame as pictures once you are finished printing with them.

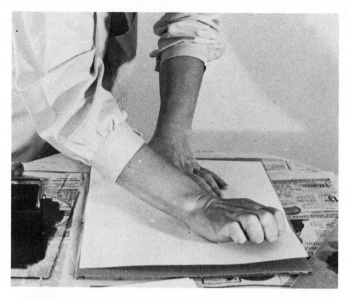

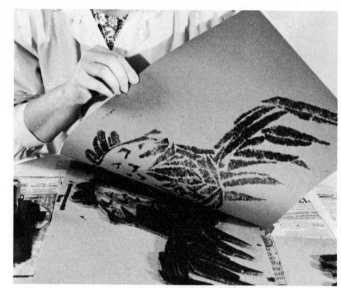

FUNNY FACE PICTURES

a collage made from nuts and bolts

WITH A HANDFUL OF HARDWARE, a bit of paint and a lot of imagination, you can make a Funny Face Picture like this. You'll find that the method is easy and the materials required are few.

You'll need a piece of plywood (or very heavy cardboard), dark household paint, a brush and an assortment of hardware such as nuts, bolts, hinges, curtain hooks, washers, nails, staples and screws.

First, place your plywood on a flat surface. Dip your brush into paint and cover the plywood from edge to edge with a thick, *heavy* coat of paint. Go on to the next step before the paint has a chance to begin to dry.

Choose some pieces of hardware—nails, hooks, screws, nuts or bolts—and arrange your picture by placing these pieces right into the wet paint. Do not move them once they've touched the paint. When the paint dries it will "glue" the hardware firmly to the plywood while, at the same time, provide a dark background which contrasts with the shiny metal of the hardware. No other glue is needed!

Let your imagination take over to create fanciful animals, beautiful flowers or even funny faces. Be sure that your collage is completely dried before you hang it up else the hardware will slide off!

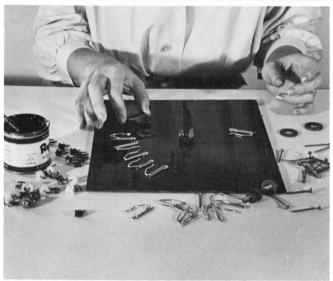

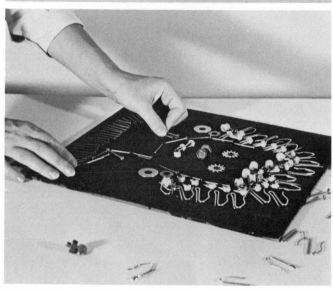

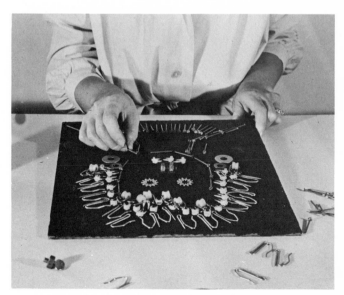

SPARKLING SPACKLE PANELS

3-dimensional reliefs made from found objects

HERE'S A CHANCE to use all those discarded things that you've saved in the garage. This project describes how to manipulate these found objects to create a really different three-dimensional panel in relief. And after you've assembled the panel, you'll be shown how to "antique" its finish so that new plastics and shiny metals suddenly look aged and worn.

You will need a stiff background such as plywood or very heavy cardboard, a box of spackle, newspaper, glue, varnish, metallic paint, a brush and some of the following objects: screws, nails, hooks and other hardware, bottle tops, string, scraps of metal and plastic.

Arrange your collection of found objects on the plywood background in any random pattern. Move the pieces around, arranging and rearranging them until they form a design that pleases you. Your relief will be especially interesting if you emphasize the thickness of objects by placing thick things next to flatter objects and by contrasting sizes by placing large objects next to smaller ones. Glue everything firmly to the plywood with fast-drying glue.

Place your hardware-covered panel on a thick pad of newspaper. Mix up a small amount of spackle, according to the manufacturer's directions. Using a large brush (or even your hand) scoop up some spackle and brush a coat of it over the entire panel. Dab on the spackle so that it covers every object well, but be careful not to drown these objects under a too-heavy coat. The effect you want is a "frosted" panel but not a shapeless relief.

If you were using plaster of paris instead of spackle for this covering step, you'd have to rush your work as fast as possible because plaster "sets up" (hardens) rapidly. Spackle will harden eventually, but it stays softer, and thus more workable, for a longer time.

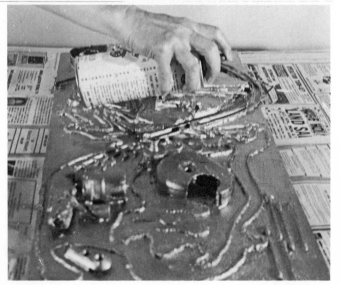

Allow the spackle-covered panel to dry for several hours or, preferably, overnight. The next step is to create a patina (finish) for your panel. An antique-like effect can be achieved in two simple steps: first, paint or spray paint the entire panel with gold, silver or copper metallic-colored paint. Allow this shiny base coat to dry. Then cover over the metal-painted panel with a coat of varnish in a dark tone. Wipe off the wet varnish immediately, here and there, with cloth or toweling to reveal tiny areas of the sparkling metallic paint below. Remove just enough to highlight parts of your panel.

In a matter of minutes, you've "aged" your work of art by at least 50 years or more!

ACROBAT TOTEM POLES

assembled from discarded bits of lumber

IN ALMOST EVERY HOUSE, at some time during the year, some carpentry is needed to improve the home's appearance or to make it more comfortable. And after that chore is finished, a lot of odds and ends of lumber are leftover to be discarded . . . or to be claimed for use by you!

If there's no carpentry going on at your house you can get similar blocks of wood by asking at your local woodworking shop. Most carpenters will be glad to give you as much as you want; otherwise, they have to pay to have such remains hauled away. The other materials you'll need are sandpaper, glue, poster paint or house paint.

The object of an Acrobat Totem Pole is not to imitate Indian or Eskimo-style totem poles, but, rather, to build a contemporary sculpture of stacked-up figures. An Acrobat Totem Pole can have as few as two figures; it can also have many more, depending on your wood supply and your ability to construct and balance the figures.

First of all, sandpaper all the rough sides of the wooden blocks. Then, stack some of them together to form a body with head, arms and legs. In constructing this Totem Pole the figures are assembled individually and then stacked together to fashion one larger piece later on.

When you have two or more figures constructed and glued together you can try different arrangements of stacking them up. Try leaning some out at angles to the others. When you like your combination of acrobats, you can glue them together into a single Totem Pole. It will be necessary to support the leaning figures while they are being glued together.

Painting the Acrobats is the next step. Keep your colors thick, especially if you are working with poster paint. Remember, you are decorating "raw," unfinished wood, which will tend to absorb much of your paint. I've found that the best method is to paint all the areas that are the same color (the skin, for example) at the same time. Use your vivid imagination to design colorful, original costumes for your Acrobats. Last, paint in the facial features which give the Acrobats expression.

If you've painted with poster paints, it's a good idea to protect your Acrobat Totem Pole against smudge marks by giving it a final coat of clear lacquer or shellac. Of course balancing Acrobats are only one of many different subjects that can be constructed from blocks of wood. Another time, why not try making animals, towns or even boats?

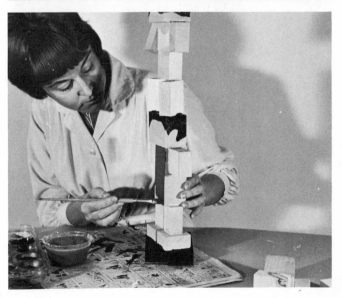

HARDWARE JEWELRY

liquid solder binds metal to metal

DID YOU KNOW that many sculptors (who ordinarily sculpt with large clay or stone forms) like to create tiny pieces of jewelry? These artists think of jewelry as small works of sculpture rather than as a mere ornament to hang around your neck or pin onto a dress. This project combines bits of hardware, liquid solder and sometimes parts of old discarded jewelry to whip up original new pieces of jewelry.

To begin, you'll need one or more of the following: the pin back from an old brooch, a chain for hanging a pendant or a pair of earring backs. You'll also need some plastic kitchen wrap, a tube of liquid solder and a variety of small bits of hardware such as carpet tacks, upholstery tacks, nails, screws, nuts, glazier's points, wire, chain or washers. You can even include some pieces of discarded jewelry, bits of colored glass or marbles. Small tweezers would be handy to have (for fussier operations), but they are not necessary.

Making Hardware Jewelry is quite simple. Begin by tearing off a small sheet of plastic wrap and place it flat

on your table. Arrange some pieces of hardware on the wrap, moving them about until their placement pleases you. Squeeze some liquid solder onto the hardware pieces to join them together. Let some of the solder flow onto the plastic wrap. You'll later discover that it will not stick to the plastic and the finished piece of jewelry can be peeled from the plastic once the solder has hardened.

Liquid solder is your most important ingredient in building this type of jewelry. It is the "glue" which holds your jewelry together and, at the same time, adds a dark gray tone which contrasts with the metals used within the pieces. As you build your jewelry, be sure to contrast tones of metal. For example, combine silver nuts with brass screws. Mix shiny tacks with dull washers. When solder is half-hardened, you can scrape it lightly to produce a bark-like texture, or when it has hardened completely, it can be polished to a shiny gloss. This new shape can be turned into a wearable piece of jewelry by adding a pin back, a chain or a pair of earring backs.

Whole pieces of discarded jewelry can also be the start of new pieces of Hardware Jewelry. Any brooch, pendant or earring can act as the base shape upon which a new surface is constructed by adding bits of hardware and "gluing" it all together with liquid solder squeezed from the tube.

Some projects ask you to work quickly and boldly. This one allows you to work slowly and carefully to create a beautiful piece of jewelry that you'd be proud to wear or to give as a present.

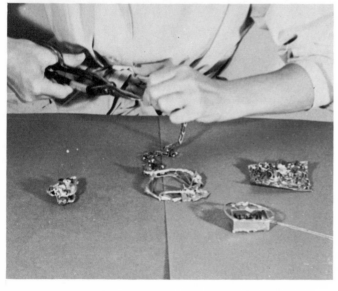

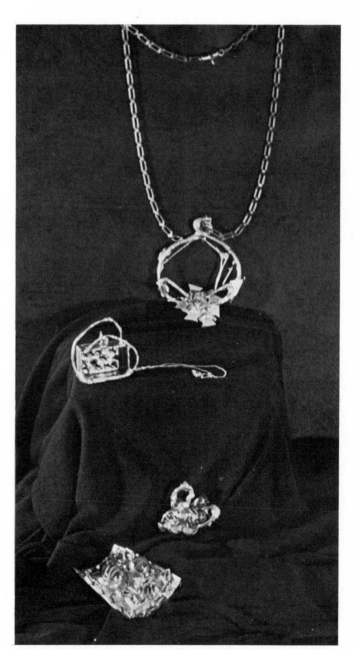

DAIRY CARTON SCULPTURE

carving from a plaster block

THERE ARE TWO basic ways to form a piece of sculpture. One is to start with a small shape of some modeling material and then to build it up by *adding* to it. The opposite way of sculpting is to start with a large shape and then to shape it by taking parts *away* from it. Dairy Carton Sculpture is the second method, for a large block of plaster is gradually chipped away, bit by bit, to shape your particular piece of sculpture.

For materials you'll need a dairy carton in any size, plaster of paris, a screwdriver or flat-edged chisel, a hammer, sandpaper and paints.

First of all, the block of plaster for carving must be cast. This is done by filling an empty dairy carton with plaster of paris. (I would advise beginners to start with a quart-size or half-gallon size carton. The more carving experience you have, the larger the container you can work upon successfully.) It will take from one to four days for the plaster to dry, depending on the size and thickness of your block. When the plaster has dried, you can tear away the cardboard carton.

The next step is to sketch the subject of your sculpture on all sides of the block. Outline your subject as it would look if you were viewing it from the sides or from the back and from the top. When these guidelines are drawn, you are ready to begin carving.

Hold a screwdriver or chisel against the areas where you want to remove plaster. Hit the end of the chisel with your hammer in a tapping-like motion. You'll soon discover that, unlike marble, plaster breaks away easily. It won't be long before you see the very rough shape of your future sculpture emerging from what once was a solid block of plaster.

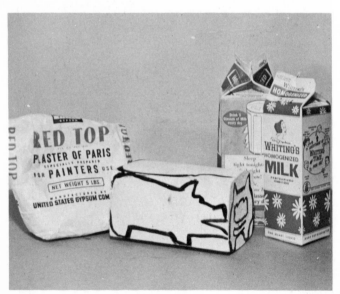

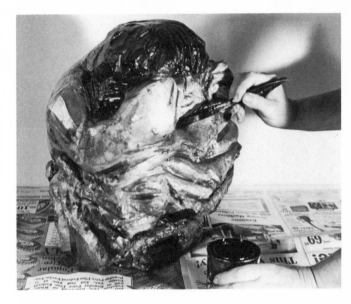

As you chip away at your sculpture, turn it frequently so that you can shape it a little at a time on all four sides. Keep chipping away until your sculpture is at an almost-finished shape. Working with plaster is always a messy business, no matter how neat you try to be. Try to wear old clothes and carve outside if possible. If you must work inside, cover your floor well with newspaper to protect it.

The final smoothing and shaping can be done with sandpaper, unless you prefer to keep the rough marks made by your chisel or screwdriver. Your finished piece can be left in its natural-white plaster color or it can be painted. When I looked at my finished sculpture, the "Stubborn Child," I decided that it would look best if I toned it with paints and varnishes.

CASTING FROM PUTTY

impressed designs are cast with plaster

THIS PROJECT shows you how to produce a design in a soft putty mold and then to reproduce this design by casting plaster in the mold. You'll find that putty is an ideal material to use for it is inexpensive, it takes a designed impression well and its oily surface does not permit plaster to stick to it.

The materials you'll need are a can of putty, plaster of paris, plastic wrap, tinfoil, cardboard, a kitchen knife, wood stain and some objects to make impressions in the putty.

First, spread the putty onto a sheet of plastic wrap which is on top of your cardboard. Roll the putty out flat so that it is approximately 1″ thick. Square off the edges of this flattened piece with a knife.

Then divide this larger piece into six or eight rectangles with a knife. Remove these rectangles from the larger piece, and place them on separate squares of tinfoil or cardboard.

Once the putty has been separated into these individual sections, you are free to travel around to different locales to take putty impressions of unusual surfaces. For example, an impression is made by pressing the putty (mounted on foil) against any interesting surface. Try taking an impression of a manhole cover, the hinge on a door or the straw on summer porch furniture.

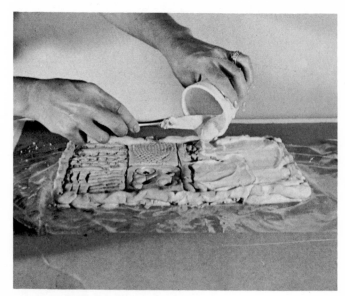

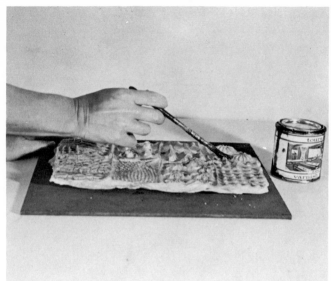

If you are unable to travel around to take such impressions, omit the step which asks you to place the putty on tin foil. Instead, use interesting things found around the garage, like points of tools, edges of hardware or bottle tops, to make designs in the separated rectangles.

Reassemble the separated sections into the original large piece. Push the rectangles together so that their sides touch and all gaps between them are closed. The next step is to build a "retaining wall" of putty around the edge of the large rectangle to help contain the plaster, which you will now use to form designs.

Mix up a batch of plaster and pour it into the putty mold to the height of the retaining wall. Allow the plaster to dry. It can then be removed easily from the putty by simply peeling off the putty mold. You'll see that the plaster has taken a perfect impression from the fine designs that you "printed" into the putty mold.

I like to tone this kind of casting with a thinned-out coat of wood stain as this helps to make the fine designs more visible.

STRIPED ROCKS

a combination of paint and stone

Sometimes, in order to fully appreciate the beauty of an object, we must focus our attention on a part of it. This project takes a single stone and uses color and paint to focus on and enhance its natural mineral beauty.

Start with a rock hunt. A short stroll along some city sidewalks or through some leafy woods should make a good beginning for your collection. Search for beautiful stones or pieces of rock that are unusual or varied in color and interesting in shape. It doesn't matter whether your rocks are rough or smooth. Besides the rocks you collect, you will also need paints, a brush and masking tape.

Study one of your rocks. Try to decide how you will divide it into painted and unpainted areas. Which sections have the most striking grain, colors, shine, speckled areas, smoothness or roughness? Are there less interesting areas which, when painted, can serve to frame the more exciting true rock parts?

When you have decided which parts of your stone are to be painted and which are to remain untouched, tear some strips of masking tape and press them onto the rock, making stripes over the area which will be kept unpainted. Each rock will probably be large enough for one to three stripes. You can use horizontal or vertical stripes, or even cross over stripes. The contours of your rock may even suggest that stripes applied at an angle suit it best.

Paint each section left exposed by the tape stripes with a different color. Select your colors to enhance the natural rock colors. For example, use shades of orange or red with pink-tinged rocks or cooler tones of blue and green with dark gray rocks. Allow the paint to dry and then peel off the tape.

If your tape has been applied to a smooth rock it will stick tight and flat against the rock. When the tape is removed, the edges of the stripes will be crisp and straight. If, however, your rock is rough and irregular, the tape edges will be loose in some places and a little paint will seep under the tape. When the tape is removed, the edges of these stripes will be furry rather than straight and smooth.

Either stripe effect is attractive, for it emphasizes the individual character of each rock . . . and that's our purpose: to make the natural beauty of the rock more clear than it was before, by selective painting.

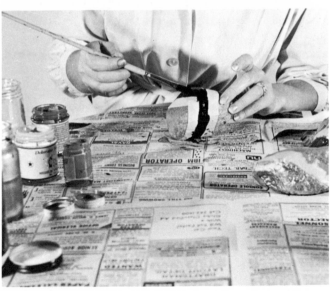

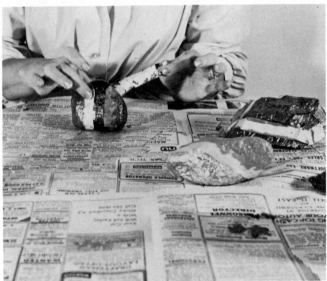

PAINTING WITH DIRT

a painting or a collage?

THE POINT where a painting turns into a collage is often very difficult to determine. Some "paintings" combine paint and paper. Other "paintings" blend paint, paper and cloth. And still others combine paint with natural elements such as dirt, sand and sawdust. These various types of "paintings" are as much a collage as they are a painting.

To begin, you will need house paint in two or three colors, pieces of thick cardboard or plywood for the background and some dirt, sand or sawdust. These natural elements can be combined with each other within a single painting, or they can be used separately in many paintings. How you choose and combine these elements depends on the textural effect you are seeking.

The technique is simple and direct. First, coat your background with a thick layer of house paint. Scoop up one of the natural elements and sprinkle or drop bits of it into the wet paint, guiding your design as you do so. Add a second color of paint if you wish. Dribble or drop paint over parts of the original paint and over some of the textured areas. Paint dribbled on top of dirt, sand or sawdust makes a crust-like surface. Paint dribbled on top of paint will cause the colors to run together. Strangely enough, accidental painting effects (like the running together of colors of paint) are often beautiful and desirable to have in a painting.

Allow your painting to dry in a flat position. You'll discover that any materials scattered earlier in wet paint are now firmly imbedded in it. These natural materials are as much a part of your "painting" as the paints themselves. Is it a collage or a painting?

RUB-IT PRINTS

from an ancient technique

STONE RUBBING is an ancient "printing" technique used by Eastern cultures for many centuries to record on paper an impression of some design or textured surface. This project shows you a quick way of adapting this very old method and it simplifies the method.

Rub-It Prints are made by placing a sheet of paper over the surface to be "printed." A dark crayon (or stick of graphite) is rubbed back and forth over the paper. An impression of the textured surface, underneath the paper, appears as you rub the crayon!

You will need sheets of thin paper (typing paper is excellent) and dark wax crayons or a stick of graphite.

Now that you are familiar with the how-to-do method, you can begin to search for surfaces to "print" with this newly-found skill. Did you know that some of the most commonplace things around us have interesting surfaces to be rubbed and recorded?

For example, have you ever taken a "print" of the cracks in the cement sidewalk? Or the bark on an old tree? Does the texture of a brick print differ from that of a wire fence? It does? Prove it! Try taking impressions of a manhole cover or a sidewalk grating. Then try to record the straw on summer furniture or the monogram on engraved silverware.

You can compose a picture out of these various rubbings by combining several prints, in an orderly way, on a single sheet of paper. Or you can even make a game of it. Ask your friends to identify objects from the rubbings. Does this guessing game sound too easy? Try it. It's more difficult than it sounds!

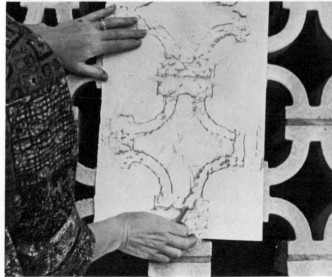

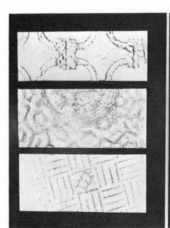

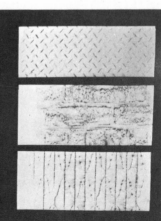

89

NATURE PRINTS

printing from leaves and weathered wood

No DOUBT you've seen hundred of thousands of leaves in your lifetime. In fact, you've probably picked several dozens of them. But have you ever thought of them as a medium of printmaking?

For materials you'll need different shapes and kinds of leaves, scraps of weathered wood, printing ink, a brayer, a sheet of cardboard for rolling out the ink, old newspaper and paper for printing.

First, cover your table with newspaper. Squeeze out some printing ink onto a sheet of cardboard. Roll the brayer back and forth in the ink until it is evenly coated. Choose one leaf from your collection (perhaps it is wiser not to start with your best leaf until you've had more printing experience), and lay it on the newspaper. Then roll the inked brayer over the whole leaf including its stem. Lift this inked leaf by its stem and transfer it to a clean section of the newspaper. Lay it down, inked side up.

Place a sheet of paper over the leaf. Rub the paper with the palm of your hand using a circular motion. This burnishing transfers the inked impression of the leaf to paper. Peel back the paper carefully and study the results of your first leaf print. Let's hope that you've gotten a perfect print. If you find, however, that your print is too faint, you need to apply more ink. If you see that the delicate vein lines are blurred and lost, you have applied too much.

It takes a bit of experimenting with inking and rubbing before you make perfect prints every time. After a while you'll know instinctively how much is the "right" amount of ink and what is the "right" amount of rubbing that's necessary to produce clear, crisp prints. Now try making some prints from pieces of weathered wood.

After you've made some good prints using one color of ink and one single leaf, you may wish to vary your results by combining inks of different colors and prints of different leaves. You can achieve some dramatic effects by overlapping prints of different colors and prints of different leaves. Try these color-design variations and see what fun Nature Prints can be!

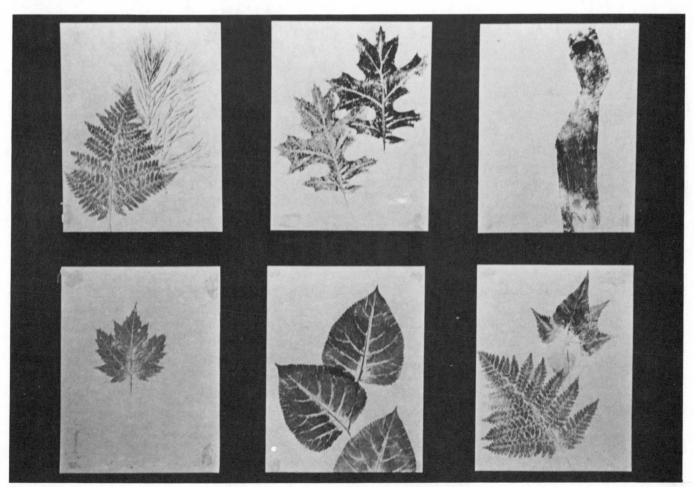

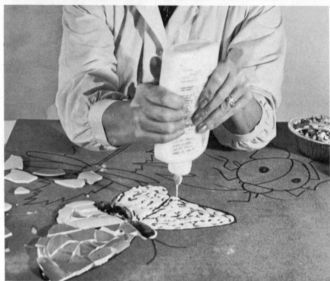

PEBBLE MOSAICS

mosaics from natural materials

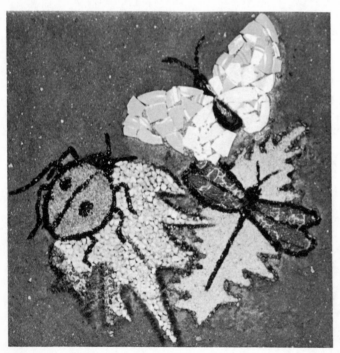

CONSTRUCTING A MOSAIC from natural materials can be as intriguing as putting together a jigsaw puzzle. You'll be amazed how many colorful and inexpensive materials for mosaic-making are waiting to be discovered around your house or backyard. If you hunt around, you'll probably turn up some (if not all) of the following materials: sand, dirt, crushed driveway gravel, seashells, pebbles, aquarium and birdcage gravel and even fragments of broken crockery. Continue the search until your collection provides you with a variety of colors and textures. Besides these natural materials, you'll need a piece of plywood for the background and white liquid glue.

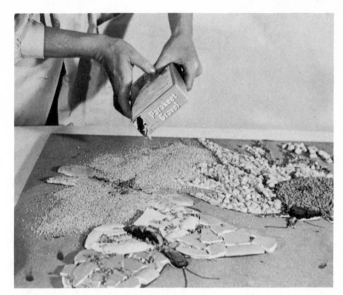

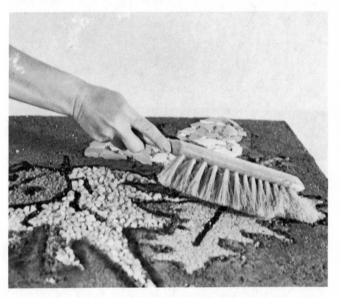

Since your mosaic-making materials are natural things, why not let nature also inspire your subject? Look around the yard or the beach or out the window. Can you see some fluttering leaves or a crawling insect? Can you spot a darting dragonfly or a crawling crab? Make any of these insects, animals or growing things the subject of your mosaic.

Draw your subject directly onto the plywood background with a dark line that can be easily seen and followed. You are now ready to start your mosaic. I've learned that the best method in making a mosaic is to fill in the subject first. I always leave my background to be filled in at the end.

Squeeze out enough glue to cover a small area of your mosaic within those drawn outlines. Fill in that area with pebbles, gravel, shells or bits of crockery, fitting the pieces carefully next to one another. No matter how perfectly you fit these pieces, the white glue will show between them. Therefore, these in-between spots of glue have to be covered up by sprinkling a fine material such as aquarium or birdcage gravel over the wet glue.

Press this fine material into the glue with your hand. Wait a few moments and then remove the excess "filler" by tilting the panel upright *quickly*, allowing the excess material to slide from the panel. You can collect this material for reuse later on.

Continue to squeeze glue, place your materials, fill in and remove excesses until the mosaic is completed, with the exception of the background. Try to contrast colors and textures within your mosaic. An unusual effect comes from using crushed seashells in one of your areas.

Reserve the sand or dirt for filling in the background. When your subject area is completed, you are ready to cover the background by spreading glue over it. Then pour a heavy layer of dirt or sand over the entire panel. Press this material well into the glue. Allow the panel to dry for a day or two before removing the excess dirt or sand.

You may find that you must "scrub" the completely dried panel to rid it of the excess material that still remains. This "scrubbing" will not harm your mosaic (if you do it lightly and if your panel is dry). It will, instead, help to uncover the beauty of your Pebble Mosaic!

FOUND GLASS COMPOSITIONS

new forms for discarded glass

A SLOW, watchful walk along a beach or even through an alleyway in the city will uncover most of the necessary ingredients for this project. The materials needed are clear and colored fragments of discarded glass, a heavy piece of wood or driftwood, a chisel or cutting device and a strong, clear glue.

Glass found at the beach is "special," for the constant changes of the tide tumble and wash the fragments until they are smooth and their edges rounded. Discarded glass (beach or otherwise) can be found in a variety of colors such as brown, green, blue, frosty white, clear and amber.

First of all, select your longest and flattest piece of glass for the base. This piece is the start of your composition upon which the rest of the glass fragments are glued. This base piece, in turn, rests in a specially dug-out channel in your driftwood base. The piece of driftwood you choose must be even and broad enough on the bottom so as not to wobble or tip over.

Chisel or dig out a 1″ channel in your piece of driftwood as long as your flat base piece of glass. Later on, your glass composition will be placed so that the base piece of glass sits in this channel which has been carved out to its dimensions.

Now you can start to assemble your Found Glass Composition. I've discovered that the best way to work is flat, on a table. This enables you to glue pieces of glass together without much difficulty. Arrange the various pieces of colored glass before you. Study the shape of your driftwood base to see if it suggests a theme for your glass work. Some pieces can be built around a specific idea, others can be, instead, a beautiful arrangement of colored glass pieces.

Your composition is constructed by adding and gluing fragments of glass to the base piece of glass, building upward and outward. Keep your entire piece under 12″ in height; glass is very heavy and there is a limit to the weight that ordinary glue will support. Overlap different colors of glass for unusual color effects. The combination of these colors will not be fully appreciated until your piece can be raised from the flat table so light passes through it.

When your composition is completely assembled, allow it to dry overnight. Then fill the channel in the wooden base with glue. Raise your composition upright into this channel. Support the piece until the glue hardens.

Now place your finished Found Glass Composition in front of a window where the light can shine through it.

SPIDER THREADS

a kind of weaving

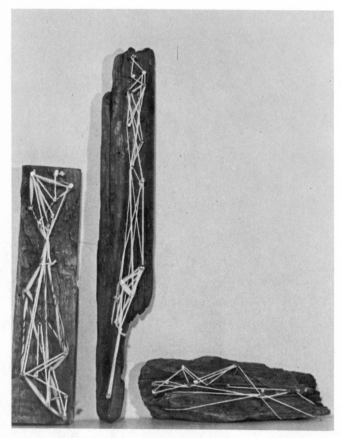

THE SPIDER starts its web with a single, fragile thread and carries it back and forth until he's woven a complicated design. "Spider Threads" imitates the spider's carrying motion, but your woven designs will be much simpler. You'll use yarn and string for your "web-making" materials and, unlike the real spider's web, your kind of weaving can be undone and woven again and again as many times as you want.

For materials you'll need a piece or two of weathered wood, string, yarn or thread and a hammer and some different-sized nails.

Begin by hammering a few nails into each of the three or four corners of your weathered wood piece. Arrange the nails so that they do not stand on soldier-straight lines and place the tallest ones in the center. Vary the number of nails in each corner.

Select a long length of string, yarn or thread. Knot one end of it to any nail and carry the string across to an opposite nail. Wind it around that nail and start back, crossing over to a nail in another corner. Wind it around that nail and go off in another direction. Weave your strands back and forth until they are used up. Always end with a knot tied in a corner, rather than in the center of your "web."

All kinds of weaving variations are possible. For example, you can combine several different types of yarn and string in one "web." You can mix colors of yarns. You can fill your "web" with a lot of weaving or a little weaving. If you don't like the results of your weaving, unwind the strings and start all over!

PEBBLE PARFAIT

rock crushing with a purpose

THIS PROJECT begins with chunks of rocks and whole seashells which are pounded and crushed into a fine gravel. The idea is to collect and arrange this gravel in layers in a clear glass tumbler so as to display the beauty and variety of colors to be found in crushed rocks and shells.

The materials you'll need for this project are rocks, seashells, fragments of building materials such as brick, slate or flagstone, a large rock for pounding, a whisk broom for sweeping up, a slender drinking glass and a wax candle for sealing the top.

To start, select any rock from your collection. Next, find a spot where you can pound this rock without harming any property. A sidewalk, a seawall or a stone stairway are good places to pound rocks. Place the small rock under the larger pounding rock and pound, pound, pound until the little rock crumbles into small pieces. Pound these small bits, again and again, until they are crushed to a fine gravel. Sweep up this gravel and pour a layer of it, about ½″ thick, into the drinking glass.

You'll soon discover that some rocks crumble easily while others refuse to break apart, even with hard pounding. Discard all rocks that do not break apart after you've pounded them once or twice. Seashells crumble very easily and they produce a powder that is nearly as fine as salt.

Choose a second rock, or even a seashell, whose color contrasts with the first rock. Pound this rock until it is reduced to a similar fine gravel. Collect this material and pour a second layer into the glass. As you pour layer upon layer, you will see them form in irregular, up-and-down patterns. Don't try to even them out. The more irregular the patterns of the layers, the more interesting the finished Pebble Parfait will be.

Continue to build up layers until the topmost one is within ¾" from the rim of the glass. Then light a wax candle (be sure an adult is present when you do) and dribble melted wax over the top layer to seal off the top of your Pebble Parfait. If you've sealed the glass tightly, the multicolored layers will not shift and mix, even if the glass is turned upside down!

FENCE WEAVING

sprucing up a wire fence

FENCE WEAVING can be very colorful or very formal. It can take a few minutes or a few hours. You can weave a fence by yourself, or you can weave one with your friends. You can weave a tiny section or a whole fifty-foot fence. You can weave it and then, if you don't like it, you can take it apart and start all over again!

First of all, the most important material in Fence Weaving is your fence. Look around until you locate a wire fence. But before you start weaving, be *sure* to ask the owner's permission! You can assure him that Fence Weaving will not damage his property in any way. It will, instead, decorate it prettily in a way that no other fence has been decorated before! Then, you must tell the owner that you will remove any decorations that you put up when you are finished. (He may ask you to leave your design!)

Besides your fence you'll need some of the following: crepe paper, tinfoil, newspaper, plastic wrap, ends of fabric, yarn, coat hangers, sticks, tin cans and string.

Choose a spot for each person to weave on that is about two feet or more wide. The weaving is done on the vertical, horizontal or diagonal lines made by the wires of your particular fence. You'll use these wires to wind various things in and out, over and under. Start by selecting one of your materials, such as a strip of colored fabric. Weave this strip through the fence in

any way that looks good to you. Tie on another color of fabric and weave this through the fence so that your weaving spot is longer or wider.

There are no "rules" to Fence Weaving, except to make the fence look as beautiful as you can. You can weave materials so that they are very close to one another or you can leave "holes" in your weaving so that you can see through it. You can dangle things like wire hangers or tin cans by tying them on with yarn or you can fill the wires with loops of newspaper. You can even crumple tinfoil or plastic wrap and stuff it between the wires. If you dangle metal objects they will clank against the wire in a breeze, adding a bit of "music" to your weaving.

After you've worked at your weaving for a while, step back away from it to see how the fence looks from a distance. Chances are, you've turned a dull, plain fence into a huge work of art!

SANDCASTING

casting plaster into sand molds

SANDCASTING is fun to do when you are at the beach. If it's not "beach weather," it's just as much fun to do at home! The directions for making a sandcasting at either the beach or at home are the same, with one exception: when you sandcast at the beach, plaster is poured directly into a depression in the sand. When you work at home, you must first put that sand in a cardboard carton and then, just as before, pour plaster into a hole (the mold) made in the sand.

For materials you'll need a deep, sturdy cardboard carton (for home casting only), a pail for carrying water, plaster of paris, a small piece of wire for a hanging hook, sand and some "tools" for decorating the mold.

At the beach, dig a hole about 6″ deep and about a foot square. At home, half-fill a carton with sand. Wet the sand well with water. Level the bottom of your mold. If you are casting at home, build up the sand around this flat bottom to make "retaining walls" to contain the plaster. (If you are working at the beach, the natural sides of your mold are your "retaining walls.")

Use your fingers, shells, driftwood, a sand shovel, a bottle cap or any object at hand to press shapes into the wet sand. You can also build up bumps and ridges. Remember that your mold is the *reverse* shape of your future casting. What is a "hole" in your sand mold is a "bump" in your plaster casting.

You can even press seashells and beach glass into the mold and leave them there. Later on, when the plaster

is poured, it will ooze around these solid pieces and they will become a permanent part of your sandcasting.

When your mold is designed, you must mix up a good quantity of plaster of paris. If you are casting at the beach, you can substitute sea water instead of the usual tap water that is needed. Pour the liquid plaster into your sand mold slowly and carefully so that the design is not disturbed. Fill your mold to a thickness of 2″–3″.

Twist a wire loop and insert it into the wet plaster for a hanging hook. Now the casting must dry. This will take a few hours in very bright sunshine or two or three days if you are working indoors.

When your sandcasting feels dry, it can be removed from its mold. Tear away the cardboard carton or dig it up from the beach. When you have freed it from its mold, you'll see that a good deal of sand still remains on its face. Carefully brush away this excess sand until you uncover the plaster. Of course, some sand always remains imbedded on the face of your casting, giving it an ancient, weathered look.